Praise for
THE ART OF BEING A STRANGER

"*The Art of Being a Stranger* is a book of such tenderness, love, beauty, and insight that I had to take a long walk before returning to its words and pictures. Once I finished and 'saw' I returned to it to 'see' again. Karen Berman is that kind of artist. I wanted to inhale this masterpiece, to carry it inside me, to stare at it as one does an amazing painting, seeing new details each time. If there is one book – not a historical treatise, but an elegy to a father and a lost world – that helps us to understand historical trauma, the frailty of religion, the horror of war, the durability of love, and yes, the meaning of living in the world today, it is this book. I am so grateful for it."

Caroline Heller, author of *Reading Claudius: A Dual Memoir* and professor emerita of education, Lesley University

"Beautiful and unsentimental, Karen Bermann's *The Art of Being a Stranger* reminds me of the timeless truth articulated by Franz Kafka: 'If the book we're reading doesn't wake us up with a blow to the head, what are we reading for? A book must be the axe for the frozen sea within us.'"

Robert Jan Van Pelt, Professor of Architecture, University of Waterloo

"Karen Bermann's gorgeously crafted graphic novel, like Käthe Kollwitz's drawings, is hauntingly evocative. It brings the sadness and glory of a twentieth century refugee family to life in its richly textured, often wildly comic mix of poetry and prose."

Jay Neugeboren and Eli Neugeboren, author and artist of *Whatever Happened to Frankie King*

"In *The Art of Being a Stranger*, author Karen Bermann tackles the complexities of her father, who was sent to Palestine following the Nazi occupation of Austria. The story of the family – poor East European Jewish immigrants to Vienna – itself challenges the tropes we commonly think of when thinking of Jewish Vienna. This family is far from the world of trips to the opera and Sachertorte. Bermann explores the difficult legacy of her father's history and parenting as she grows up in New York City with a parent who wrestles constantly with his dark past. This heavily illustrated novel delves with honesty into the nuances and pain the past has laid, through her father, on all of them."

Michael Simonson, Head of Public Outreach and Archivist, Leo Baeck Institute

"The warp of Nazi hatred and the weft of Jewish fury have seldom been woven into such a singular fabric. The author evokes her father with constant exasperation and profound underlying affection; the juxtaposition between his rage and her forgiving sadness manifest in both word and image, makes a strange Haggadah. *The Art of Being a Stranger* is different from all other books in its combination of apparent simplicity and deep insight into a tragedy that will forever be unfolding."

Andrew Solomon, *New York Times* bestselling author and winner of the National Book Award, author of *Far from the Tree* and *The Noonday Demon*, and professor of psychology at Yale University, University of Cambridge, and Columbia University

THE ART OF BEING A

A FAMILY MEMOIR

WRITTEN AND ILLUSTRATED BY

KAREN BERMANN

New Jewish Press
An imprint of University of Toronto Press
Toronto Buffalo London
utppublishing.com

Library and Archives Canada Cataloguing in Publication

Title: The art of being a stranger : a family memoir / written and illustrated by Karen Bermann.
Names: Bermann, Karen, author, artist.
Identifiers: Canadiana (print) 20250200627 | Canadiana (ebook) 20250203847 | ISBN 9781487565275 (softcover) | ISBN 9781487565268 (hardcover) | ISBN 9781487565299 (EPUB) | ISBN 9781487565282 (PDF)
Subjects: LCSH: Bermann, Karen – Family – Comic books, strips, etc.| LCSH: Bermann, Fritz – Comic books, strips, etc. | LCSH: Parent and adult child – Comic books, strips, etc. | LCSH: Parent and child – Comic books, strips, etc. | LCSH: Generational trauma – Comic books, strips, etc. | LCSH: Comics artists – United States – Biography – Comic books, strips, etc. | LCGFT: Biographical comics.
Classification: LCC HQ755.86 .B47 2025 | DDC 306.874/2 – dc23

ISBN 978-1-4875-6526-8 (cloth)
ISBN 978-1-4875-6527-5 (paper)
ISBN 978-1-4875-6529-9 (EPUB)
ISBN 978-1-4875-6528-2 (PDF)

Printed in Canada

Cover design: Karen Bermann, Megan Lueneburg, and Sebastian Frye
Cover image: Illustration by Karen Bermann
Page design: Karen Bermann, Megan Lueneburg, and Val Cooke

We wish to acknowledge the land on which the University of Toronto Press operates. This land is the traditional territory of the Wendat, the Anishnaabeg, the Haudenosaunee, the Métis, and the Mississaugas of the Credit First Nation.

University of Toronto Press acknowledges the financial support of the Government of Canada, the Canada Council for the Arts, and the Ontario Arts Council, an agency of the Government of Ontario, for its publishing activities.

Canada Council for the Arts
Conseil des arts du Canada

Funded by the Government of Canada
Financé par le gouvernement du Canada

For my sister, Arlene

CONTENTS

ACKNOWLEDGMENTS

My deepest thanks go to:

Diana and Malachy McCourt, beloved friends, fellow travelers, and role models who have nurtured me with tenderness and boisterousness (and Guinness) for many decades. They helped this book come to light, and they helped me come to light.

Murray Weiss of Catalyst Literary Management, my agent, a kind and generous person, who patiently and devotedly worked on behalf of this book, who kept the faith and told me to do the same (and I did).

Megan Lueneburg, multidisciplinary designer, muse, essential assistant, digital wizard, and codesigner of this book.

Isabella Clough Marinaro, Paolo Livorati, and Chiara Sophie, my Roman family, for support and love, for close reading of infinite drafts, for infinite gin & tonics in and out of lockdown, and for everything, really.

Rebecca Coffey, brilliant science and humor writer, artist and designer, and great critic, who guided me through all the forests and swamps, practical and existential, of this project.

Mary Bisbee-Beek, independent publicist, fierce and kind boss of creating order and making things happen.

Stephen Robson, publisher of Fanfare/Ponent Mon, who believed in the book and stuck his neck out to help me when we'd never even met, because why? Well, there are such people in this world.

My deepest thanks to the entire team at the University of Toronto Press for their dedication and expertise in bringing this book to life. Special thanks to Stephen Shapiro and Mary Lui, my editors, for their insightful guidance and patience; Val Cooke and Sebastian Frye for working with us on page and cover design, respectively; Vesna Micic and Stephanie Mazza in the marketing department for their dedication in ensuring this book finds its readers; Aditi Parikh, my enthusiastic and super-capable go-to-for-everything person at UTP. Perrin Lindelauf for his creative copyediting of messy two-voice poetry-prose issues. Big thanks too to the rest of the UTP team.

For reading and commentary and other gifts of time and kindness, I thank Arlene Bermann, Paolo Buatti, Debra Gold, Thyrza Nichols Goodeve, Rachel Lopez, Consuelo Nuñez Ciuffa, Sarah Plotkin, Jennifer Terry, and Isabella Zani. And in Vienna, Marianne Schulze, human rights lawyer, friend, and ally, on behalf of everyone, for everything.

VIENNA
1922–1938

What a magnificent panorama 1

Fritz, my father, says:

Look at that! What a magnificent panorama!
I always felt at home in the mountains.
I loved wide-open spaces.

As a kid in the Boy Scouts, we climbed in the Alps.
We rotated and peed in three countries at once.

"When was that, Dad?"

That was 1932.
Before the end of the world as I knew it.

I lived with my parents and my brother and sisters,
Leo, Dora, and Elsa, in the second district of Vienna,
officially Leopoldstadt, unofficially Mazzesinsel,
Matzoh Island, where poor Jews lived.

We kept kosher, we went to Jewish schools,
we never left our neighborhood
or mixed with the goyim.

My father Josef came from Galicia,
in the eastern part of the Austro-Hungarian Empire,
from a miserable Jewish community filled
with poor and ignorant people.

And in this town, which was already full
of the most miserable poor people,
my father's father took care of the bodies of the dead.

He was the washer of bodies,
the job reserved for the poorest
and most miserable person,
a kind of untouchable.
He was illiterate.

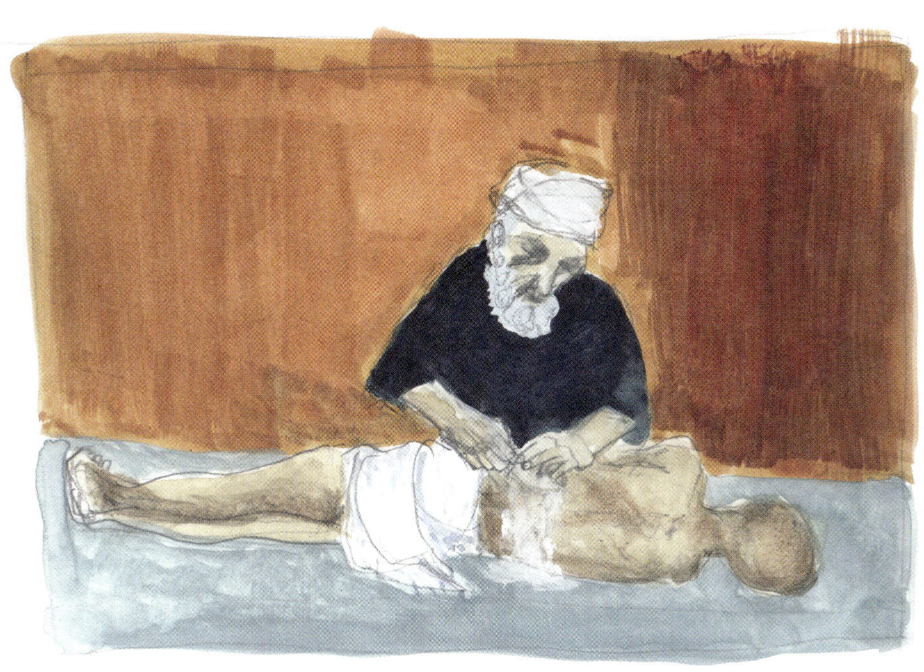

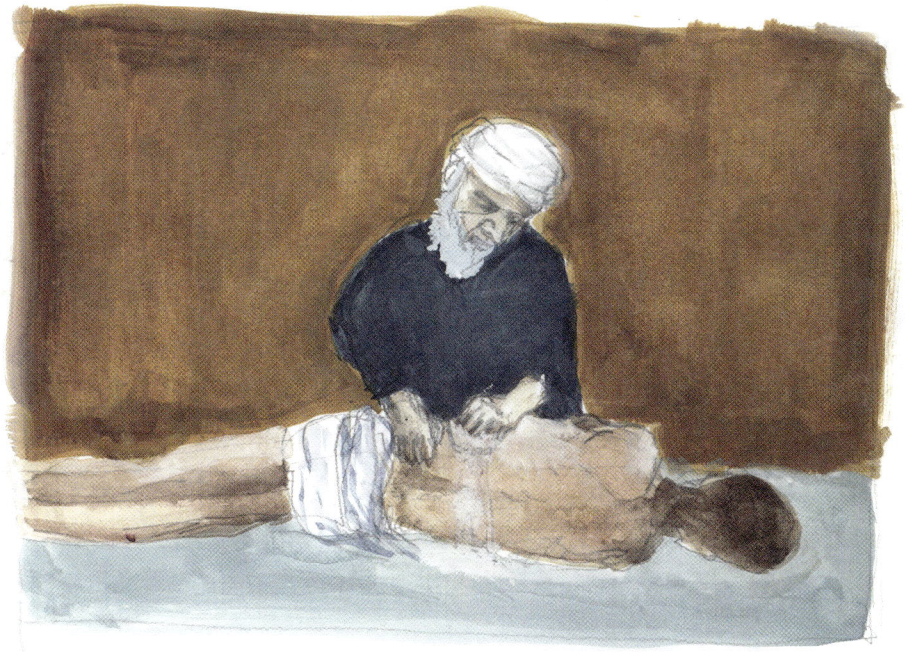

Unlike his father, my father Josef was semiliterate,
not that he ever read anything except for
his religious books. He and his two brothers,
they wanted to be somebodies.
They made their way to Vienna
and set up shop in a textile-making business.

They spoke Yiddish and a poor German,
the German of peasants from the eastern lands.
They were always afraid of being laughed at.

But once my father came to Vienna,
he didn't speak Yiddish anymore.
And he always wore a suit.

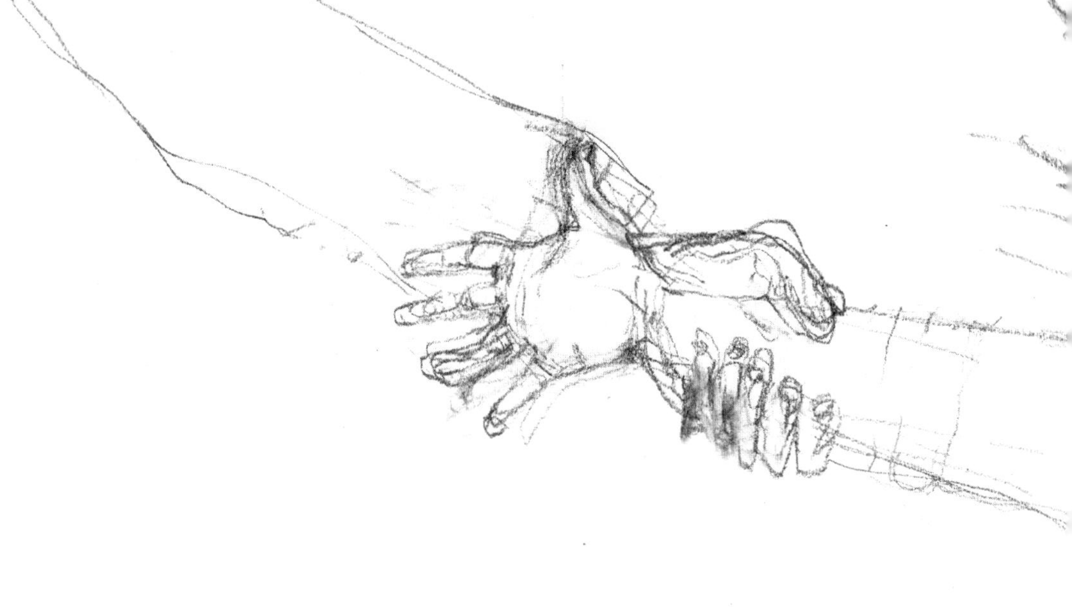

Josef, in his suit,
always wanted to be a proper Viennese,
and so he was very happy to have a marriage arranged
to my mother, Melanie, who was from
a somewhat assimilated but still religious family,
proper Viennese, very middle-class.
She was the rant of the litter, so to speak –

"RUNT, Dad – "

the runt of the litter,
the youngest, and she was deaf in one ear
from a childhood illness and was often sick.
But she was a lively, thinking person,
she loved to be with people,
to listen to music, to read, to laugh, and
she didn't want to have anything to do with my father Josef,
who was really a boring religious guy, ignorant, rigid,
with traditional ideas about women,
without a sense of humor.

She resisted, she fought.
She had a boyfriend of sorts.
He was a painter, a bohemian, a Jew of course,
but not religious, and of course her father
wouldn't let her marry him.
He had no money.

Years later, when my parents, Melanie and Josef,
lived in Flushing, which was full of people
of their background, they met someone
who had known the painter till his death.
He'd survived the war and never married.
He said he could never marry anyone but my mother.

"Do you believe that, Dad?"

How should I know?

A religious Jew couldn't smoke on Shabbos.
This drove Josef crazy.
Any little noise we children made he would go wild
and take off his belt.
Then he went to his synagogue and prayed
like a pious man of God.
This was how I began to hate religion.

My brother Leo took after my father,
but my sister Dora was a freethinking person
like my mother, and she introduced me to socialism.
In this way were formed my fundamental ideas to this day.

Jews were not allowed to smoke on the Sabbath. So he beat his children instead.

I was always in trouble when I was a kid.
When I was ten or so, about your age,
we were requested to write a story in class.
I wrote that I was going to build a bomb and
bring it to school and blow the whole place
to kingdom come.
My mother was called into school
to talk about the threats her boy was making.

"Oh, Dad, that is really bad."

Yes, that was a particularly bad one.

"Were you always so angry?"

I was born angry. And scared. As was my father before me.

"Even before the Nazis, you were so angry and scared?"

Well, yes. But the Nazis didn't help.

Already I knew that God did not exist

In February 1934 in Vienna there was shooting in the streets.
It was civil war between the socialists and the military.
The prelude to fascism.

I was eleven.
My mother made me stay home many days.
This was even before she made me stay home
for fear of the Nazis.

During the gunfire
I used to sneak out to play football
in the park near our house.

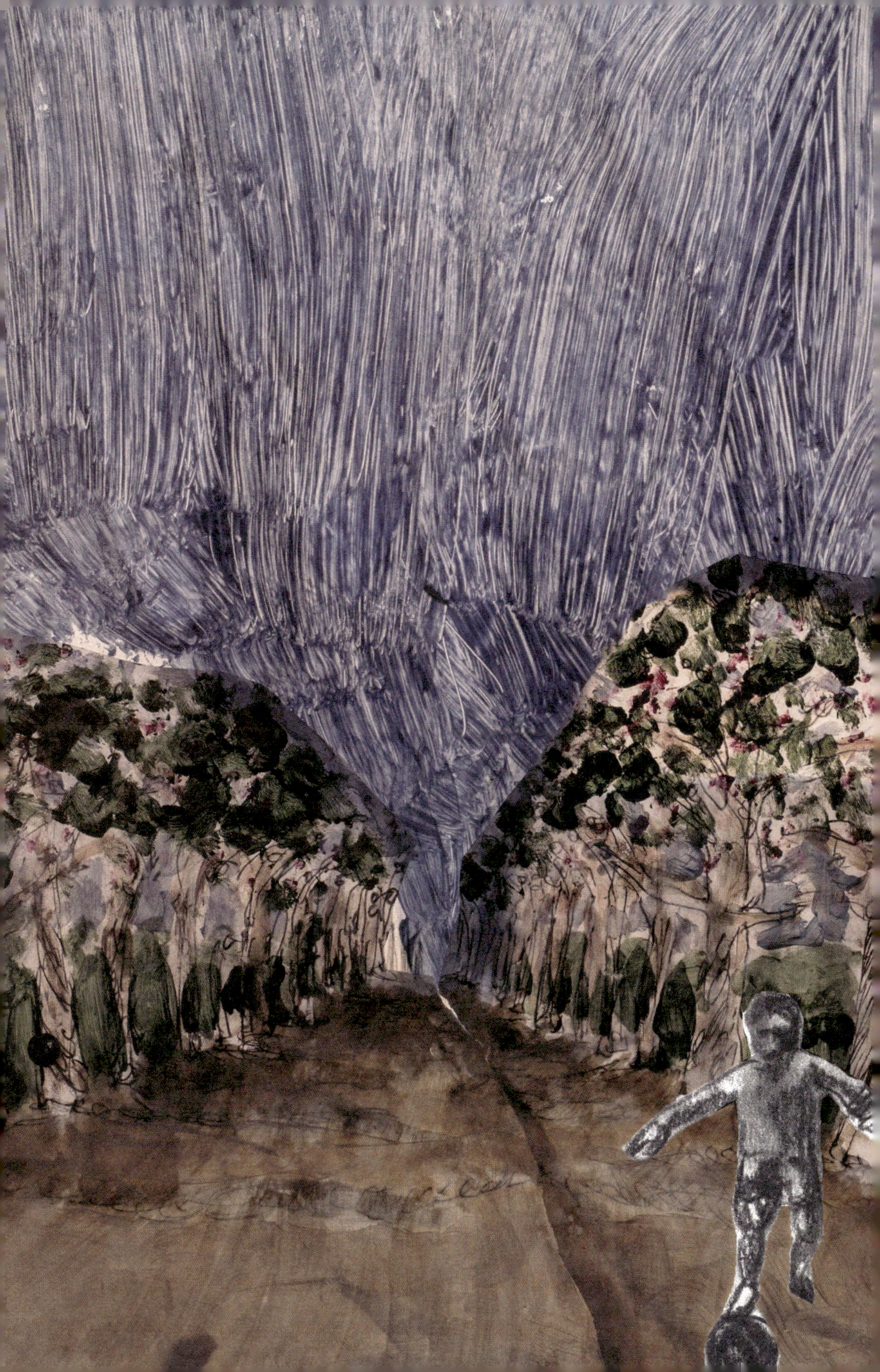

We heard that there was an open confrontation
at Karl-Marx-Hof. It was workers' housing,
a stronghold of socialism.
There was artillery fire.

I knew the place well.
My sister worked there as a kindergarten teacher.
I jumped onto a streetcar.
I hid in the bushes and saw all the fighting.

So there was fear and uncertainty in the streets,
and in our lives, even before the Nazis came.

My father sat on his bed with his head in his hands. My sister Dora told my parents it was time to go, but he couldn't move.

He kept repeating, "The British won't let anything happen. The Americans won't let anything happen." It was 1938.

"What about God not letting anything happen?"

Well, my father was certainly praying. Me, already I knew that God did not exist.

Some were galvanized,
some were paralyzed.

Some knew,
some did not know.
Some knew
and did not know.

It wasn't until Kristallnacht when they made him kneel and clean the street that Josef understood it was time to leave.

The tourist Vienna, the fantasy Vienna,
the Vienna of those other refugees in New York
who were rich and assimilated and are still complaining
about leaving behind their pianos – the Vienna of their
precious sachertorte, their music lessons, their skating
rinks, their sugary, insipid, antisemitic waltzes –
that is not the Vienna I knew.

The Vienna I knew was a shtetl of poor religious Jews,
a ghetto of ignorant bastards who beat their children
for making noise on Shabbos, but who knew,
who knew in their bones that they were not welcome,
who recognized the stench of antisemitism in the street
while others were perfuming their noses in the rose gardens.
So who were the ignorant bastards in the end?

My mother took us to the train station very early in the morning.
My sister Elsa and I, with our little valises.
The train had grilles on the windows to protect us from attack
as we passed through the Austrian countryside.
Such was the climate at that time.

On that train we were all kids,
Austrian Jewish kids leaving their parents behind.
The little ones had no idea what was going on.
Neither did I, really, though it had been explained to me.
At fifteen years of age I was still a baby.

And I had to be responsible for my young sister,
ten years of age, who came with me on the trip.

We were lucky to go on that train. I know that now, of course,
but I did not feel at all lucky on that day.
And I could not make sense of it for my sister
when she asked where we were going.

My mother bought me a big heavy black leather coat for the trip.
Why she gave me a black leather coat to go into the desert
I'll never know.

PALESTINE
1938–1948

Black leather coat

When we got off the boat in Haifa we waited for our names to be called. My sister Elsa and the other children too young to work were taken away to an orphanage.

An elderly couple, Russians, came forward for me. They took me to their farm in a remote part of the country. They had no children and they had decided to take in a refugee child to help them.

We drove a horse and buggy for many hours. That is how I found myself for the first time, a city boy in a black leather coat, milking a cow at four o'clock in the morning.

The Russian farmer and I started work at four a.m. and quit before noon. We would come in, have lunch, and then the farmwife would bring out a giant samovar filled with boiling tea.

"Drink." We drank. – "Have another glass." This went on till we had had maybe ten little glasses of tea. The heat built up inside my body till I thought I would die, and then I would explode in sweat and feel a blissful relief. I would totter to my bed, fall down, and sleep like the dead till the late afternoon.

The Russian couple were kind to me. They treated me like a son. They would have liked me to regard them as family. But I could not. Had I done so I would have had to entertain the idea that my own parents were gone, that I would not see again my own parents. This was a disloyalty I could not do. It was an idea that could not be considered. I had no idea where my parents were, and I did not hear from them for many years, but still, it was unthinkable.

So although I was just a kid, and alone, I kept my distance. And when I was eighteen, I took my black leather coat and left the farm to go live on a kibbutz among other young people.

A dog-or-eat-the-dog world

We young kibbutz men were employed by the British to evict Bedouins from their land. They gave us guns and sent us into the desert with long, fancy, official letters explaining that the land had been purchased and that the Bedouins could no longer graze livestock on it. Of course, aside from the fact that they couldn't read the letters, this made no sense to the Bedouins, who had been on this same land a thousand years. They were nomadic; the concept of land as property had no value to them. And an explanation that a rich man in Paris had sold the land to the British, who intended to make it part of a new country? It was completely abstract, it was absurd, it was cruel.

We could see all this very clearly. We did not feel good. But we were assigned a job to do and we did it.

According to their custom, the Bedouins had to receive us graciously as guests. Of course they knew what was happening. Everyone knew what was happening. But still custom had to be observed.

So they greeted us with ceremony and kindness, we went into their tents, we sat with them, they served us lamb, they poured us tea, and we delivered our eviction letters.

It's true what you say. There is a certain symmetry to it. We were pushed out of our homes, and we pushed other people out of their homes. But – it was us or them.

If I can teach you only one thing about this world, my dear child, it is this:

It's a dog-or-eat-the-dog world.

"You mean dog-eat-dog world, Dad."

I mean you do not want to be the dog that gets eaten.

It's a
dog-or-
eat-dog
world.
Do you
understand
me?
Do you
catch my
meaning?

NEW YORK
1948–2013

Remember me, Charlie?

My first job in New York I worked for this guy
Charlie Voelker. A German. I saw the ad in
the New York Times. *They needed a handyman.*
When he hired me, he thought that I was a German too.
When he told me he spent the war on a submarine,
I didn't tell him I spent the war on a kibbutz.
I needed a job.

He interviewed me, he said, You speak German?
I said, Yes.

He hired a landsmann, *so to speak, or so he thought.*

He was a Nazi soldier and then he married this
American woman and here he was, so help me God,
the superintendent of the Hamilton,
on the corner opposite the Times building.

It was a good-size office building. He hired me, and
I started to work as a handyman. I fixed windows,
whatever a handyman does. He hired me, and I could do
no wrong.

Not only that, when some other repair guy was stuck
with a job, he would call me over, show me off, say,
Fritz can do that.

When Yom Kippur came, I could not NOT take off.
It was unthinkable to go to work on Yom Kippur,
even if just for the sake of the parents.

Universal
Elevator

For the two months previous I was his showpiece.
I kept my mouth shut. I needed the job.
Then came the holidays.
I walked in – I had the foreboding already.
I don't know why I told him the truth.

I said, "Mr. Voelker, I'm taking off tomorrow.
It's Yom Kippur."

He was sitting in a chair like this, one of these tippy chairs that rock back, and first he couldn't speak, and then he said,

"FRITZ! FRITZ!
NOT YOU, FRITZ!!"

– and he leaned back as far as the chair would go and started to tip, so I ran over and caught him.

He didn't say anything else, but from that day on whatever I did was wrong. I could see the handwriting on the wall.

"Writing on the wall, Dad."

After a few days I started to look for another job.

And indeed he fired me and gave me two weeks' notice. By that time I was a union man, and he couldn't fire me on the spot. In those two weeks I found another job at Williams & Company.

Then over twenty years I rose in the ladder of Williams
to being the head of the Maintenance Department.
Three hundred giant commercial buildings in Manhattan.
Somehow from being a peasant in Palestine I found myself
a big shot in the world of New York building maintenance.

I was moseying along as good as I could, minding
my own business, until one day when Jerry Cohen,
the son of the boss of Williams – of course Williams
wasn't their real name – told me that he was taking
a sailing course.

He said, "This bastard instructor is giving me a hard time.
I suspect he's a Jew-hater. This bastard, Charlie Voelker."

It came back to me.
In my vicious mind I saw the possibilities.

So I went up to see this guy Voelker after all these many
years, and I said, "Charlie, do you remember me?"

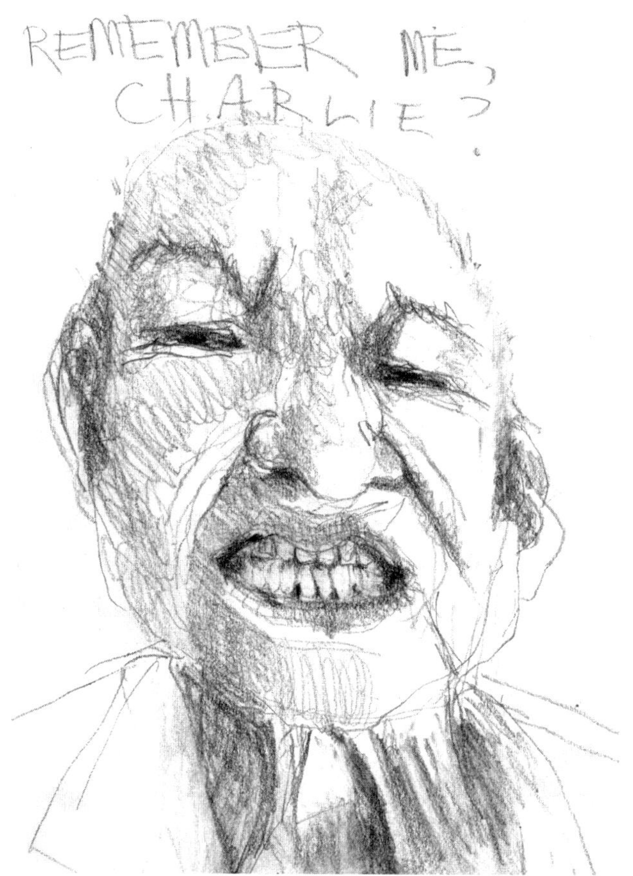
REMEMBER ME,
CHARLIE?

I said to him, "You're running a sailing course on East Eighty-Sixth Street, aren't you? You're giving this guy Cohen a hard time, aren't you? You know, Charlie, that's not a very smart thing to do."

I said, "You fired me, Charlie, but now the tables are turned. Now I'm a big shot in building maintenance. Now I can get you fired. You're an old guy looking for your pension, and I can get you fired in a jiffy. You know, Charlie, if you don't pass this guy, give him his sailing license in a hurry, I'm going to get you fired."

I saw it dawn on him what I was saying.

I said to him, "Charlie, remember what happened between you and me? You fired me because I was a Jew. Now I could get you fired because you are a Jew-hating German. I could get you fired like you fired me, but I won't do that, because Jews don't do that, because I am not a bastard like you, a German bastard like you."

"I'm a Jew, I'm a human being. You're a pig, you're a monster, you're a German. Typical German. Nazi."

He said, "Oh no no no."

Cohen told me right away, "Bermann, what did you do? This guy was so sweet to me ..."

I said, "I just went up and talked to him."

That was it. I said to him, I said, "I could get you fired, Charlie. You're a German. You're a bastard."

And he said, "Oh no Fritz – "

I said, "That's right, Charlie. It's me, Fritz. Remember me? Now the tables are turned, aren't they, Charlie?"

I could see the lightning dawn on his face about who I was and what was what.

He said, "Oh no, Fritz – "

"ENOUGH, Dad. That's ENOUGH."

Jerry Cohen said, "What did you do, Bermann? This guy was sweet as pie – "

And Voelker said, "Oh no Fritz ..."

Building maintenance 1

I worked with the Rosenwachs.
They made the best water tanks in the city. Still do.

I had to put a big water tower on top
of one of the Lillian Wald Houses.
I managed to shut down the FDR Drive
and put a crane on it.
In the middle of the night
we lifted this giant water tower
fourteen stories.

When I was doing elevator installation, I got a call for a top-secret job.

> "What could possibly be top secret about elevator installation?"

In New York, plenty.

This job was to replace the elevator that went directly into the apartment of Helena Rubenstein.

I was escorted by her private security in every minute because she wanted gold elevator buttons.

There was a rumor that she had a bathroom with solid-gold fixtures.

Even the toilet seat.

I had friends in the Highway Department too.

"What do you mean by friends, Dad?"

In my business, in the business of building maintenance
in New York, you made friends with cash, honey.
That's how it worked.

The New York that you people know,
the New York of museums and operas,
is not the New York that I know.
Mine is a New York of crooks giving and taking bribes
on construction sites, of filthy stairwells
in public housing projects
where we were instructed to carry
a flashlight and a gun,
and even filthier kitchens in
high-class restaurants.

You know that New York is full of creeks and rivers
forced underground. So one day I get a panicked call
from a tenant downtown.

"The basement is full of water!"

I get down there quick and big surprise. I said to him,
"Why do you think it's called Spring Street?
Where do you think names come from?"

There's a city, a whole invisible city, under this one.
It asserts itself. It cannot be driven under completely.
It erupts everywhere.

All maintenance men know this.

The projects

When your sister was born we moved to the new New York City Housing Authority projects in East New York, in Brooklyn, when all around was still undeveloped marshland. At the edge of the projects was a working farm.

One evening coming home from work I was almost run over by a horse that had gotten through the fence and was running wild among the buildings and parking lots.

In the early days of living in those big projects us fathers would come home from work and get off the elevator on the wrong floor and try to put our keys into the wrong doors – we were so mixed up by the enormity and the sameness of it. There was a special NYCHA blue
that was everywhere: the tiles in the lobby, the elevator doors, the elevator buttons.

Then over time things changed: floors began to distinguish themselves by the different cooking smells, we recognized the differences in views, trees began to grow and acquire distinct characters, and so on.

In the beginning it was great: two big clean bedrooms, planes taking off, a nice view of Idlewild.
That's JFK now.

Then things started to break down.
I remember carrying you up eleven stories. Of course, there was a lack of maintenance from the start.
That's always the story, honey.

Though Fritz sometimes had to carry me up eleven flights of stairs,
I loved living in the projects.
I especially loved being so near the airport.
I stayed at the window to watch the planes take off.
The fourteen-story buildings had blue lights atop them
to warn the planes, the same beautiful blue lights
that lined the runways of the airport.

At night in our beds all across the projects, Linden Houses,
while the adults washed dishes and talked, kids stopped breathing
when the planes flew across our rooms, striping the floors, the walls,
the terrain of our bodies under the sheets.

Then there was the plane in Jacques and Dora's living room.
We called Jacques, who had married Fritz's sister Dora in Paris,
French Uncle Jacques in honor of the Frenchness
he valued above all things.
He'd been a pilot in the French Resistance
during the war. He walked over mountains,
he told us; he escaped from a Spanish jail.
He had carried a tiny vial of cyanide so
he could kill himself by cracking it in his teeth
before betraying what he knew if captured.

In 1965 Jacques started building a little plane in
the eighth-story apartment in Queens next to the
Throgs Neck Bridge. It was a French plane, of course,
from a French plane kit company, with parts that came
by mail from France. His plan was to build the body
first, then the wings separately, then to have the
living room windows removed and a crane
put on the roof to hoist the parts out of the building.

But the French airplane kit company failed, and
the wing parts never came. We forgot about them;
really we forgot that it was a plane. We leaned against it
and put our chocolate cake on it. A giant plant that
sat next to it and had already grown to the ceiling
began to grow horizontally. Leaves and branches
drifted over the plane.

Jacques dominated the table, raving about the superiority of all things French, or about a scientific invention that he was working on – perpetual motion, antigravity – while Fritz protested and grew frustrated and disgusted.

He shouted, *Talk sense, Jacques!*
Jacques shouted, "Fritzie, you will see!"

Jacques was obsessed with the beautiful engineering of the Mercedes-Benz and the tragedy of it.

Because one did not purchase so much as a tube of Nivea from the Germans, may their economy therefore collapse and they be condemned to live in the ruin they brought upon themselves, those bastards.

This was the only thing Jacques and my father agreed on.

It's not a question of IF but of WHEN

My father said,

Honey, don't walk on the metal doors that open up onto basements! Hinges! The potential for failure!

And I don't.

Remember what I've always told you:
Why have such blind faith?
Do you know the guy who did the installation?
Do you know the guy who does the maintenance?
Are you sure there IS maintenance?
Are you sure some crook isn't putting cash into his pocket right now, being paid off to not do the inspection that would lead to the necessary maintenance?

These do seem like perfectly good questions.

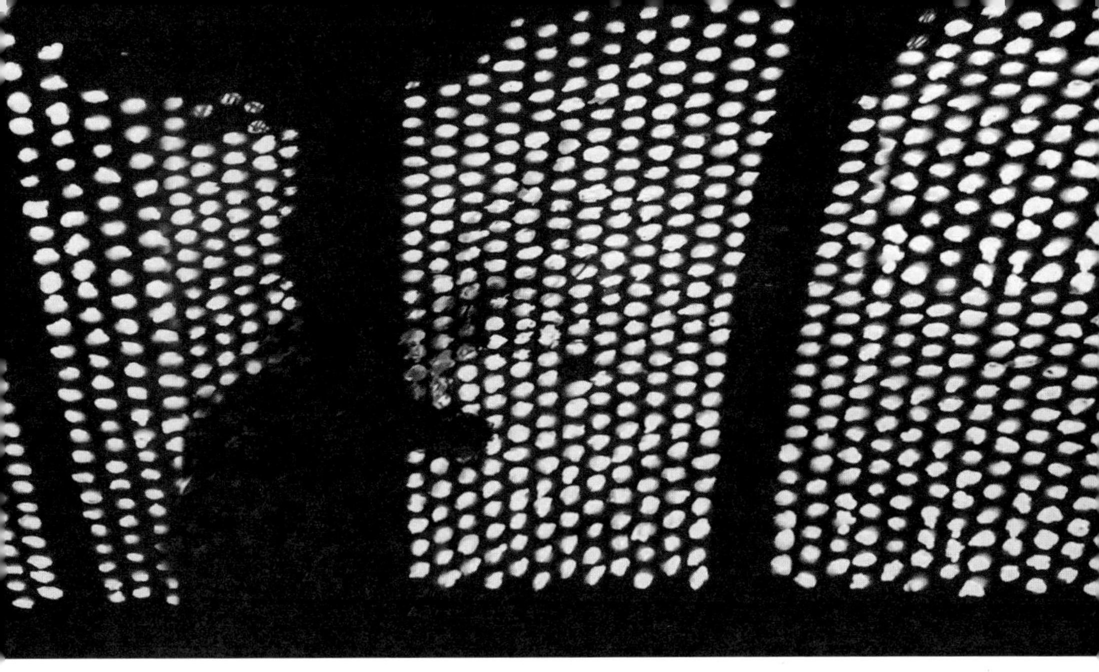

“Your father is so paranoid,” my friends said,
to which I opened my mouth then closed it again.
Good for them, keeping on the sunny side,
always, etcetera.

But I also avoid the places where round glass
blocks let light into basements.

> *What’s that? Cement grout? Are you kidding?*
> *It doesn’t hurt to be too careful.*

Actually, I could argue with that.
It *does* hurt to be too careful.
He was hurt into being too careful,
and he hurt me into being too careful.

> *I’m a good maintenance man because I know*
> *it’s not a question of IF, but of WHEN.*

A good maintenance man was an understatement.
Fritz was a famous, a great maintenance man
in New York.

He told us incredible stories: about boilers exploding,
about fire escapes pulling away from walls,
about reinforced concrete without reinforcement.

There is a photo of my father on the morning in 1938
that his mother put him on a train
full of children leaving Vienna,
with his pale, unformed, uncertain face.
He wore his mother's parting gift,
the oversize black leather coat, and he always said,

> *Only God knows why my mother gave me a giant*
> *leather coat when I was on my way to Palestine.*
> *To the desert.*

I know why:
She must have thought of it as a shield, a strong housing
around more fragile interior parts, something that would
protect and resist, a second skin, a place to hide,
a show of strength.

> *I'm a good maintenance man because I know*
> *that things are always about to fall apart.*

MY MOTHER BOUGHT ME A

BLACK LEATHER FOR

My father said,

You ask if it was interesting working all those years
in New York building maintenance.
Was it interesting?

My dear child, do you know what I would like?
I'd like to have a giant bulldozer as wide as
the island of Manhattan.
I'd start at Battery Park, and I'd work my way up,
flattening everything in my path ...

My New York is a place where people will do anything
for a buck.
Ground zero of capitalism, belly of the beast,
a savage place that destroys more lives every day
than could be destroyed by anything but
an atom bomb,
forget my pitiful bulldozer,
an atom bomb, which I personally
would gladly drop on Manhattan
with my own hands,
which is why I could not cry big crocodile tears
when the World Trade Center was destroyed –

"DAD!"

My dear child, this is a savage country.

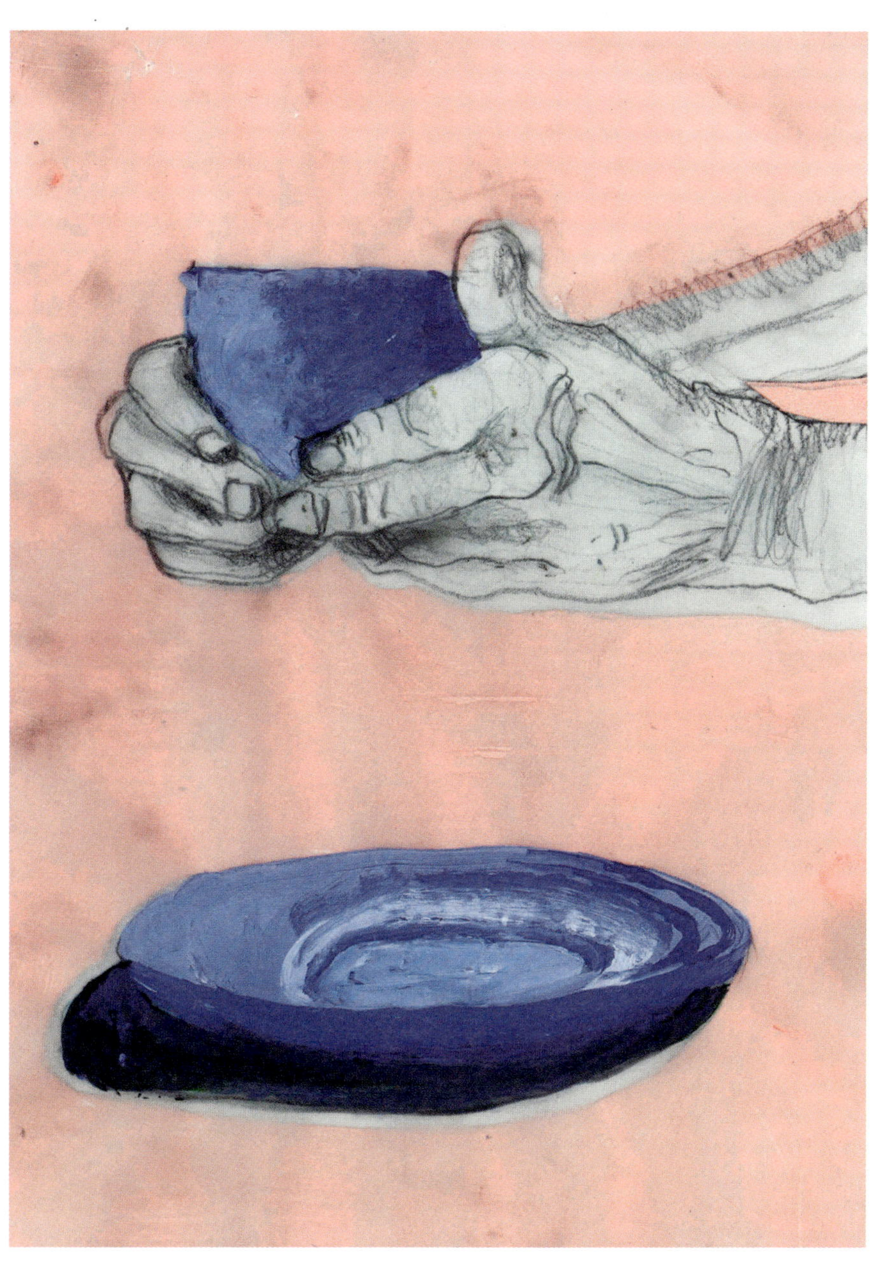

Secure in the knowledge
that I am a stranger

My father said,

What was so desirable about a house in Queens?
That's what everyone wanted, so I assumed
there must be something very good about it. Look, first
you got married, and everything else just followed.
Did I want kids? I can't answer that.
I didn't consider the alternative. I had no time
to think in those days. I was busy with other things.

PROUDLY
SERVING
QUEENS
SINCE
1963

When those Girl Scouts come to the door
I send them away pronto. Never mind the cookies.
You get your cookies somewhere else.
That's a paramilitary organization.
It makes me sick to see a child in uniform.

Don't you dare go to a demonstration.
We could all get deported.
You don't think so?
You think being the child of naturalized citizens,
they won't deport you, too?
Honey, everything the Nazis did was legal.
You are as naïve as an American.

Queens, land of new homeowners, proud and frightened,
who had just gotten out of somewhere or something
by the skin of their teeth and were now being American
with mid-sixties vengeance.
Armed, girded, the houses wired with burglar alarms,
with movement sensors on the lawns,
the floodlights illuminating, sometimes,
in the middle of the night
a terrified rabbit –

> *In this chair I am content to sit for the rest of my life.*
> *In this country I am secure in the knowledge*
> *that I am a stranger.*

He pushed back in his black Naugahyde recliner
while the needle dropped on Beethoven's *Pastorale*
loud enough to be heard over the lawnmowers.

I asked my mother if a baby could be born and nobody know about it. A secret baby.

> "Well, it would be very difficult. Maybe in the beginning, OK, but then the baby would have to go to the doctor at some point, get vaccinated, go to school to learn how to read … "

"No no," I said. "No doctor, you take care of it at home, you teach it to read at home. You hide it from the neighbors, even. This baby grows up and it becomes a secret person. There is no record of its existence. It's totally free."

> "I don't think it would feel very free. I think it would feel the opposite of free."

But nobody could come for it. Nobody could take it away.

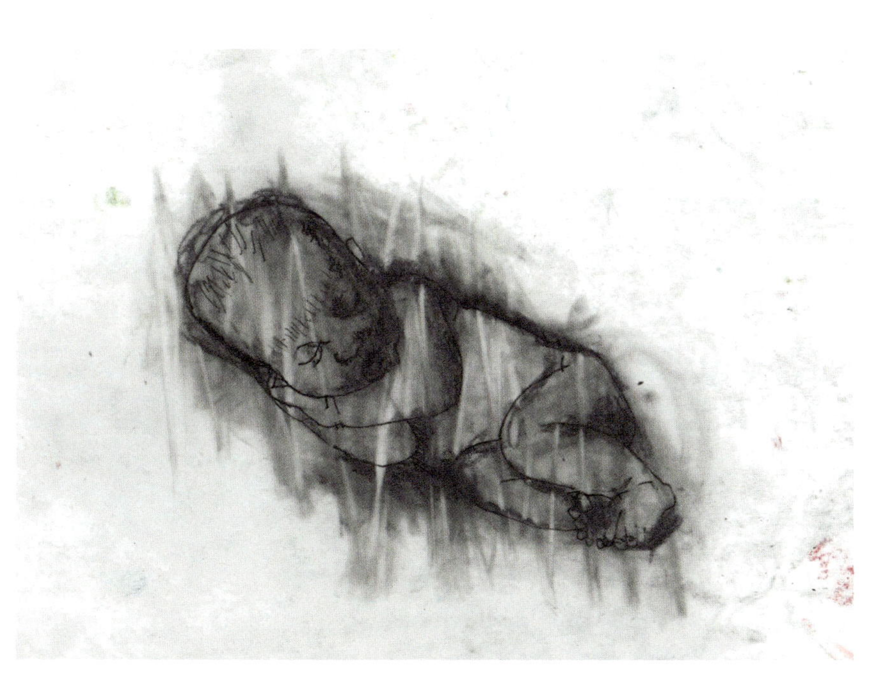

Riding the subway, I saw a family eating dinner
deep underground.

In an incandescent room, the mother stood
and put food on the plates.

Later, they sat around a giant radio together.
I had seen pictures of radios like this.

The children didn't go to school; the adults didn't go to work.
They never left their home deep underneath the city.
They were totally safe there in the yellow light.

Almost nobody knew they were there except for me
because I knelt on the rattan seats watching inside
every subway tunnel, watching for them, with my mother
gripping my waistband, my hands filthy from the filthy
windows, the rattan carving grooves into my knees,
and I wasn't going to say anything.

Made for the ear of God

We went to the Palisades in New Jersey every year
on Yom Kippur, on the High Holy Days, to not offend
the neighbors, who did not drive on the holidays,
who fasted and prayed and went to synagogue.
We left very early and came back very late.
We climbed the rocks overlooking the Hudson all day.

Whether my father cared about offending religious neighbors,
there was some sense of ritual still there.
Some vestige of loyalty.
Of belonging, and not wanting to be cast out.

It was his High Holy Day too.
Mountains were his ritual and his religion.

My father said,

My dear child, stop whatever you're doing.
Sit down on the couch and listen.
Get a cup of tea and sit down.
And take an untertasse *so you don't drip on the couch!*

This is what I will hear when I reach
the gates of Paradise.
This is the essence of the divine!
This is everything that is sacred!
This is music made for the ear of God.

> "What are you talking about, Dad?
> You don't believe in God or any of that stuff."

I make an exception for Beethoven.

My father said,

Somewhere along the line during the war my young sister Elsa
faked her age to get out of that orphanage in Palestine
and join the British Army. She drove a supply truck
through the desert. She met a South African soldier,
not Jewish of course, an Afrikaaner of all things,
and got pregnant, so they had to get married.

When they got the news after the war, when letters and
news began to get through, my father and my brother
immediately disowned her. They hadn't seen her since
1938, they weren't even sure she was alive, and when they
found out she was, did they rejoice? No, instead they sat
shiva for her, the full seven days. She never had contact
with her father Josef again.
He gave her up to the dead.

You want to know about violence?
Religion is the root of all violence.

I oppose myself to religion completely also because, as a kid, while I was in the men's room in the temple eating a secret cube of sugar because I was about to faint from hunger from fasting, thanking God on Yom Kippur for keeping me alive for another year if he please would, to spend another year at the hands of my father, that brutal, savage, bigoted, religious bastard, waiting to see if God's hand would kill me for I don't know what, fervently trembling, praying in the synagogue, begging God for forgiveness for I don't know what, and all this bullshit –

All this time, my mother wasn't even allowed to participate in this sacred bullshit.
Women weren't good enough for it.

No, I will not go into a synagogue.
My mother Melanie, who because of illness in childhood
was forced into a marriage by her father,
who was the victim of a husband who was a bastard,
a victim of her time and place.

Do you know that at her funeral my brother brought in some Orthodox rabbi who didn't even know her to talk about her and what a good religious woman she was, and I kept my mouth shut, even though I wanted to shout that as soon as my father died she ordered a ham sandwich in a diner, just for the hell of it, because she was a lively person full of curiosity even though she was old, and also for spite. And now she is buried alongside that horrible husband in a place that hates women and was eulogized by a man who didn't know her and praised her as a woman of valor for having raised four Jewish children.

I won't go into a synagogue.

It's my last protest for my mother, the pains of her life,
and now forced to spend her eternity in a strange place.

My grandmother Melanie always wanted to tell me stories and she tried, but she had very little English. I understood one: about the spherical pastry dipped in chocolate and injected with whipped cream that she ate in Vienna at the afternoon *jause*. It broke apart in your hands, a fragile shell, a sweet cloudy interior, explosive. They ate it with such greed and pleasure like there was no tomorrow.

This was their brittle, disappearing world.

I would have liked, she would have liked,
to dress me up and take me there
to eat pastry with her.

Bone by jeweled bone

Fritz wouldn't go to a demonstration, but he gave money to progressive organizations and to people on the street. He gave money even when he didn't have money. There but for the grace of God go I, he told me.

Never mind the God part, honey,
just understand the principle.

At every opportunity he'd take his
American Civil Liberties Union membership card
out of his wallet and wave it around.

Since 1954!

"What about Skokie, Dad?"

All his friends had turned away from the ACLU when they defended the right of American Nazis to march in Skokie.

Sometimes you have to hold your nose
in order to do the right thing.

He wanted to leave a big chunk of money to the ACLU.

Honey, I can trust you girls to do this when I die?

"Of course, Dad."

Some things are sacred.

So the ACLU was also sacred.

He was furious when he found me struggling to eat hot soup right-handed while his father held my left hand behind my back. He was done with the cruelties of his old world. He believed deeply in defending the weak.

This was true, and it was also not true.

I had my teeth drilled without Novocaine.
My father said it wasn't really necessary.

> *It doesn't hurt that much.*
> *People make a big fuss about a little pain.*

He said some people just say, "No, thank you."
I wanted to be that kind of person,
the kind of person he was.
I said, "No, thank you." I gripped the chair arms.
Tears leaked from the sides of my eyes.

> "Because you're in pain," the dentist said.

"It's just from the effort," I said.

I worked to control the contractions in my body so that
they wouldn't jolt the drill.

> The dentist stopped. "Please let me – "

"No, no, it's OK."

> And again – "This is crazy," the dentist said.

"It doesn't hurt that much!"

And I went back to my gripping and suppressed shaking.
Finally, he threw the drill down. Now he had tears in his
eyes and was shaking.

> "I can't work like this. What's wrong with you people?
> I'm not even going to finish. Go to another dentist."

So I surrendered.

He gave me a shot of Novocaine. The drilling proceeded.
I was light, near-ecstatic from the cessation of pain.
My God! I had no idea that one could choose it.
To not have pain.

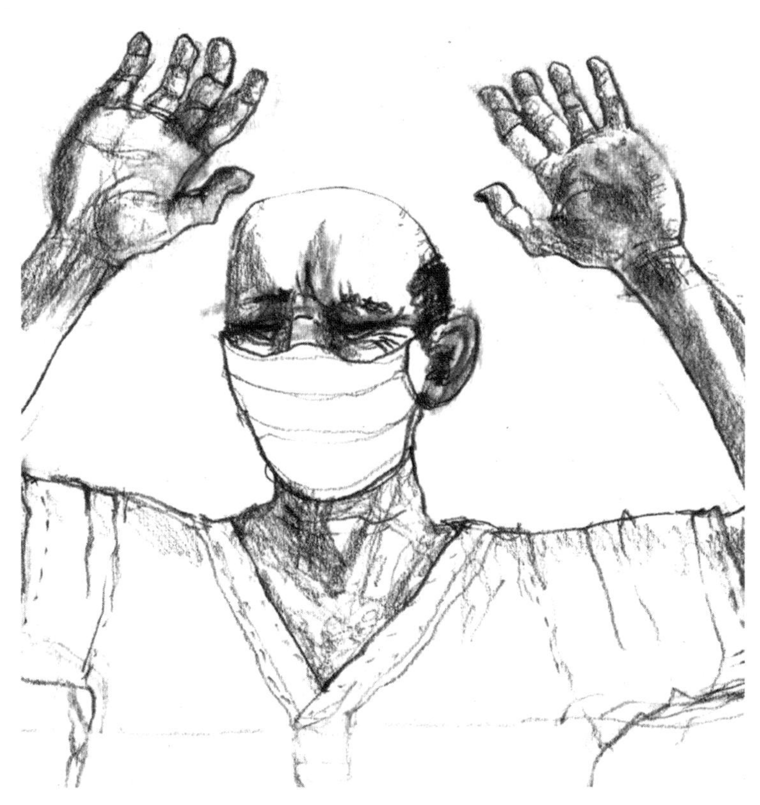

My father arrived at the door to my room one day
with screwdriver in hand.

> *I told you no closing the door. So now, no door.*
> *You want alone? I'll give you alone!*

I stayed alone in my room for two weeks,
bent over my pink record player.
"To everything, turn turn turn."

He'd said he'd break my backbone.
The backbone-of-my-resistance.

"Your father's such a Nazi," my teenage American
friends said, and I said, "Don't say that,"
because it was so wrong,
and because of its unspeakable truth,
the common truth of the fathers.

Breaking backbones-of-resistance,
that's what they did, those fathers.
Not like their fathers did,
with belt and strap,
not with their hands,
but with their bodies as they backed you down the hall
one step at a time,
till you couldn't back up anymore,
till your back was against the wall.

And with their voices, their hot eyes,
their teeth, gritted teeth, chopping teeth,
as if he'd break my bones with the
little bones of his mouth.

Some of us were galvanized, some were paralyzed.
Some were galvanized then and paralyzed later.
Some resisted only to later break
their own backbones-of-resistance.
Some raged and tried to escape.
Some played dead to stay alive.

I built a parallel structure to the one I lived
in my father's house. In secret, in my room,
in the days of my confinement,
facing away from the open doorway,
facing the corner window where I could see
the city in the far distance,
I built my parallel existence.

At least in this I could not be stopped.

I built it when I rode my bicycle as fast as it could go,
watching intently, in the blur of the street, for a new
landscape to open up in a crack between houses.
Then I'd disappear.

I built it on the bus at night, way in the back
with the sleepy junkies, looking out into the darkness.

I built it with every dangerous chance I took
and choice I made, because danger was my right.

My resistance was my existence.
I built it, bone by jeweled bone.

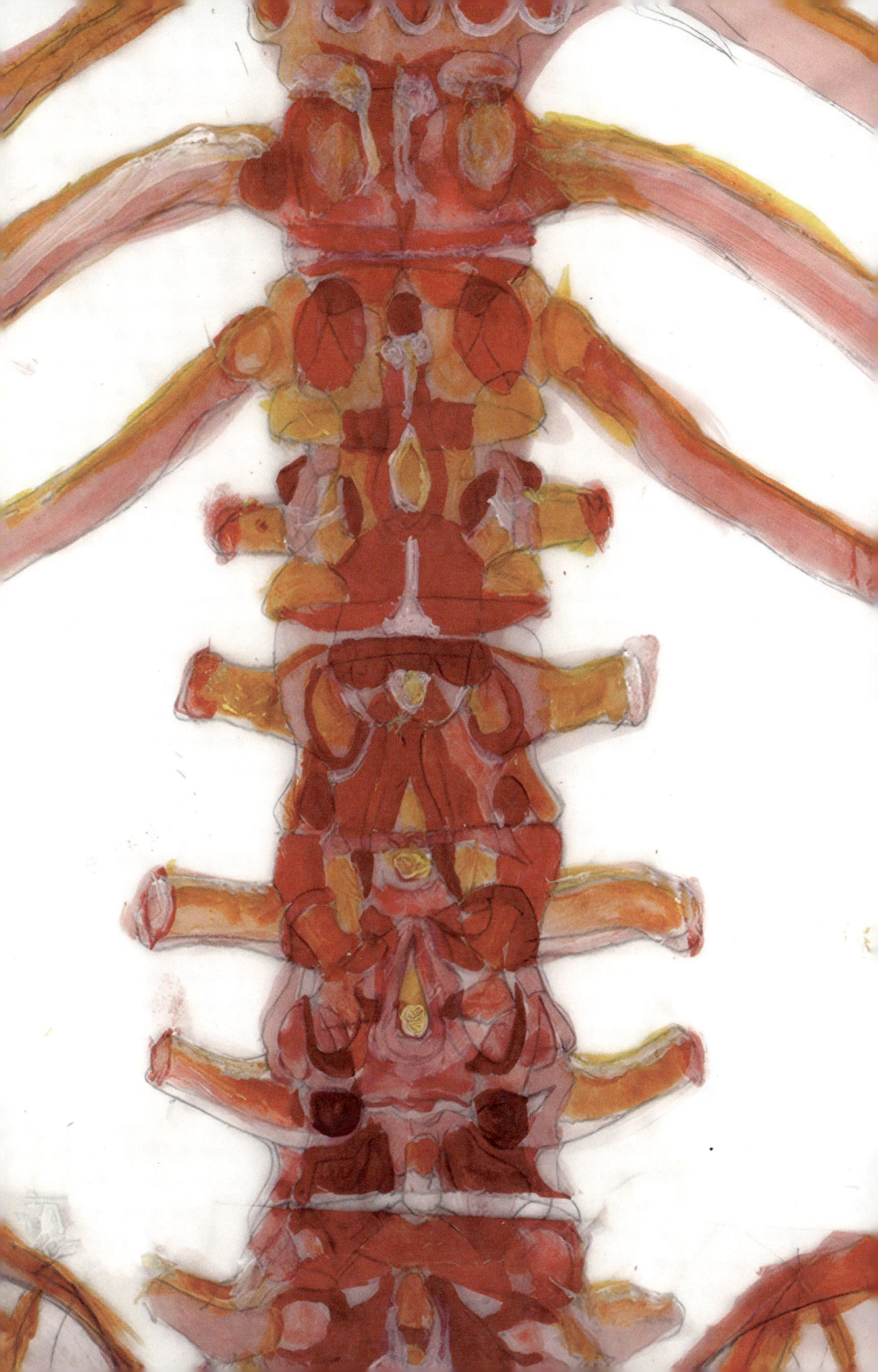

A wall of forgetting

My father said,

Yes, I went back to Vienna, once, 1986.
My then-girlfriend dragged me there.
She thought it would be therapeutic.
I told her, "I need a big therapeutic bomb
to drop on a bunch of countries."

On the train to Vienna, a German fellow
stepped on my foot.
Big strong healthy young guy.

I said to him, quietly, so no one could hear, in German,
I said: "Whatsamatter, fella, didn't you hear Germany
lost the war?"
Just like that I said it to him. I said, "Whatsamatter, you
didn't hear? You didn't hear Germany lost the war?"

I said it in German, very quiet and vicious-like.
"Hey fella, whatsamatter?"
I told him, "Didn't you hear Germany lost the war?"

"Hey, fella?" I said it to him just like that, I said, "Hey,
whatsamatter, fella, you didn't hear – "

"ENOUGH, DAD, I GOT IT."

"What, you didn't hear? Germany lost the war."
I said it to him. In German I said it to him, I said,
"Hey, fella, didn't you hear? – "

WENT BACK ONE TIME B
A WALL OF FORGETTING

I wanted to see my old house in Vienna,
the apartment building where I grew up,
where I played in the stairwell,
where we watched the prisoners take their walks
in the back of the police station in the courtyard.
I went back once. But I felt nothing.

A wall of forgetting separates me from my past.

In our grandparents' tiny apartment in Flushing
the children are gathered at one end of the table,
and the adults are at the other, speaking German.
We know to ignore them. Our parents don't speak
German with us, only with each other for the sake of
the grandparents, who even after thirty years don't
really speak English.

We have always known that speaking German
was scheduled for obsolescence in the same way
that the grandparents were, old and not of this world.
It was the language of National Socialism, of all the sadistic
fathers. But, I thought, it's also your mother tongue,
and how can you do without that voice, those first words,
basic and necessary as a spoon?

But German was on the other side of the wall of forgetting.

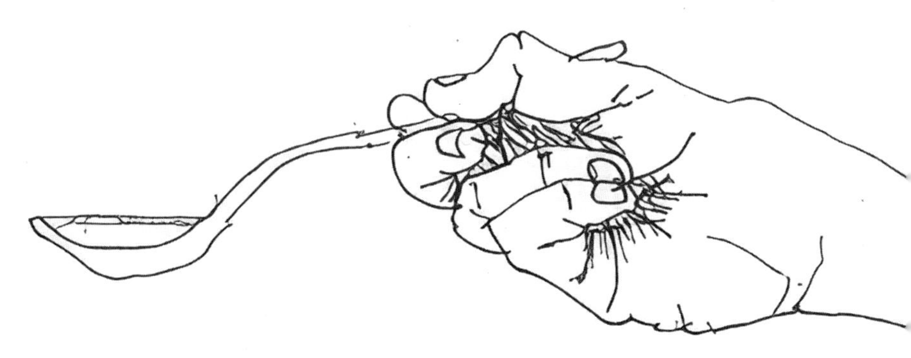

Fritz was ruthlessly (one of his favorite words)
honest about the danger of hope.
Hope was more than pointless, it was stupid, and led
to suffering. People disappointed by life
were stupid people; they made him angry.

He thought it would be all honey and roses!
Well, he woke up but good!

They had been taken in, they got took,
and so they suffered. We would be the smart ones,
smart and strong enough not to be taken in.
He taught us about the strength of character
that hopelessness required.

It was the lesson of the vial of cyanide.
Don't let them take you.

My father said,

I'm sorry to have to inform you of this, my dear child,
but let it never be said of me that I was not honest
with my children,
that I gave them pie in the sky,
that I told them like these innocent Americans
who don't know anything about the world,
who don't know history, not even their own,
that they have control over their lives,
that happiness is waiting for them,
that they can become anything they want to become.

Who ever told you life was fair?
Who ever told you you deserve?
You make the best of what you got.
No one can ever say I sugarcoated things for my children.

I tell my children the truth, even when it is brutal.
I tell my children the truth, because *it is brutal.*
I tell my children the truth:
It doesn't matter how good you are, or how smart you are,
or what you want,
or how hard you try.

History is a tidal wave and it will wash you away.

My sister is traveling alone in Europe.
My father calls me.

> *Are you crazy? What will happen if she falls down and breaks her leg? Who do you think will help her? She doesn't speak the language. No one will help her. You think she can count on a policeman? You kids don't know nothing about policemen and how they operate.*

"Dad, she has a credit card, she has a cellphone, she has resources, she will get help."

> *You children are so naïve it's incredible. What country, what world, no, what universe did you grow up in?*

"Not yours, Dad."

> *That's what you think.*

"Dad, she is a tourist, not a refugee."

My father said,

I should never have stayed in the US.
It's not the place for me.

"But what is, Dad?"

Good question. What about you?

"Good question.
But I like it like this."

Wouldn't you feel more comfortable if you
settled down somewhere?

"I don't want to feel more comfortable, Dad.
I like being uncomfortable.
Uncomfortable is my homeland."

He never said “survivor.”
I didn’t either.
I too was ashamed before the children whose
parents had numbers on their arms.
I felt unworthy of my bad dreams.

Building maintenance 2

My city was stitched together by numbers, dates, stories. Especially stories.

> *Where on West Twenty-Sixth does your friend live? At 31 West Twenty-Sixth I took care of a giant flood on New Year's Day in 1964.*
>
> *When you go to work, please walk on the south side of the street. I happen to know a lousy pair of basement doors just west of Ninth Avenue. I knew the bum who put them in.*
>
> *Southwest corner Forty-Ninth and Lex, a splendid lobby! Very high-quality elevators, too. The best technology you could get in 1965. They spore no expense.*

"SPARED, Dad."

The infinite litany and library of addresses. I ran my finger along the buildings as I walked down the streets, touching their faces and their golden spines.

In 1974 there were over a thousand abandoned buildings
on the Lower East Side. Ditched by landlords who
couldn't squeeze a profit out of a tenement in need of
heat, in need of maintenance, a building that leaked
from every weak pore.

I was nineteen. A group of us took one of these buildings
from the city. We took it into our care. It had been
burned thirteen times before the last tenants left.
519 East Eleventh Street, between A and B.

We entered it in silence, listening to its silence.
O its broken bones.
O its blackened spine.

The first principle of building maintenance is enclosure.
A building open to the elements is a building in exile
from itself. It's a contradiction in terms.

One needs a strong housing to protect a fragile interior
against the elements. I learned this from the boy
with the black leather coat, who had been open
to the elements.

We washed the faces of the brick. We supported
the floors with jacks and made them level again.
We built out, filled in, lined, aligned.

We got up on tall ladders and wire-brushed the beams
before the city inspector came to stick the metal
extension of his wooden measure into the char.

> "Less than a quarter of an inch!"

He wrote it down on a form from the Buildings Department.

> "The beam stays!"

Everyone smiled, including him. He'd taught us this trick.
The char in our eyes, in our mouths.

At lunchtime, on a scrap of sheetrock or wood, I wrote
a weather report, what we'd accomplished that day,
who, numb with cold, had hit his thumb with a hammer.
Then I'd drop in my Coke can and the front page of
the *Post* and close up the wall. The wall cavity,
narrow space of containment, hiding place, is where
I left word.

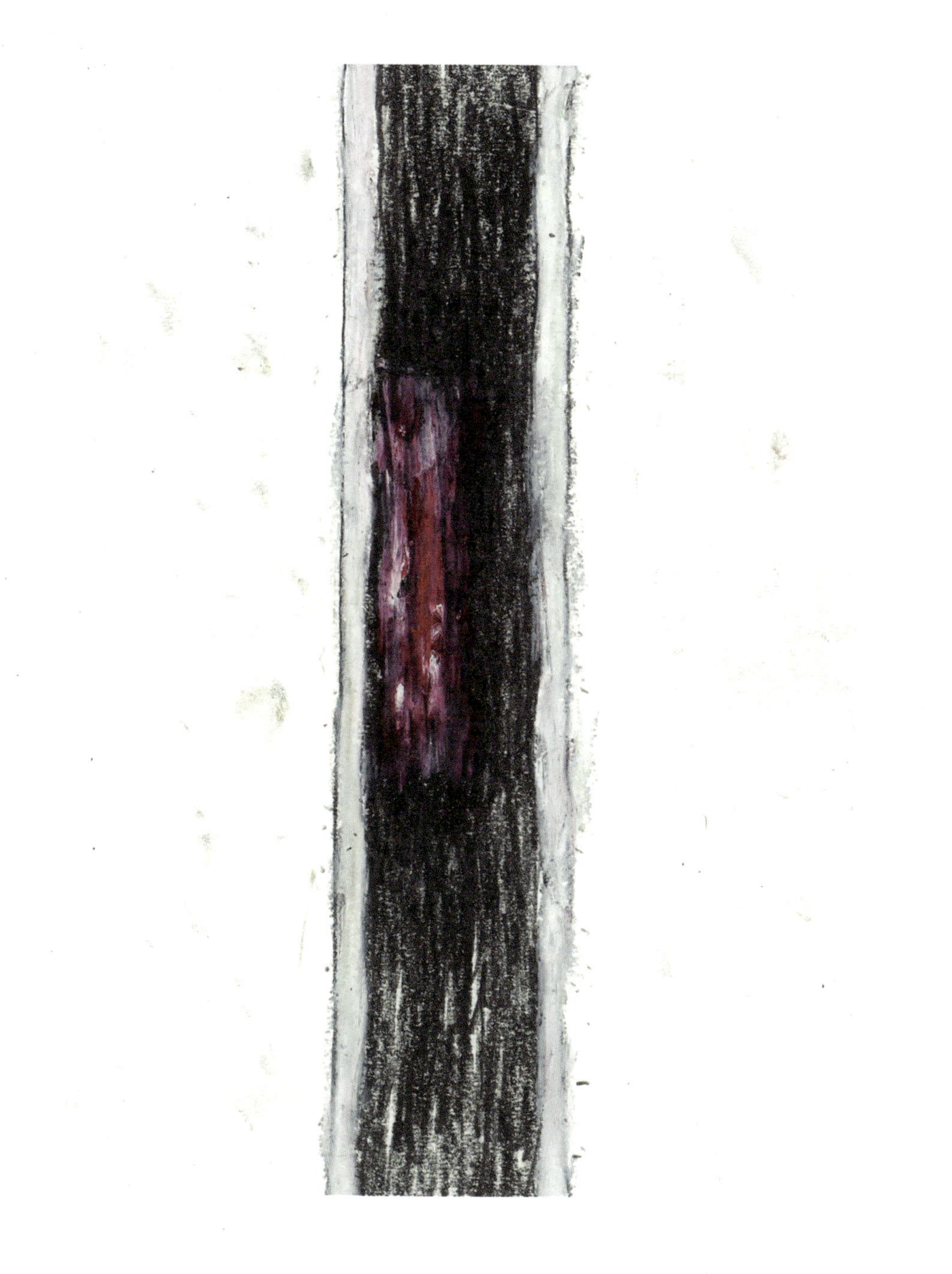

While I was working sweat equity at 519 East Eleventh,
Fritz was installing elevators in the Christadora House
around the corner for our enemies, the gentrifiers.
I admired his name written in script on the pocket
of his workshirt when he stopped by.

Guys would yell up, "Karen, your father's here – "
I climbed down six precarious stories. They stood
around on the sidewalk smirking and winking
while he berated me.

> *You were on the ROOF? God in Heaven, what did*
> *I do in my life that was so terrible that I deserve*
> *to see my daughter, a nice Jewish girl from Queens –*

(and Brooklyn, I'd remind him, don't forget Brooklyn)

> *– up on the roof of a burned-out building on the*
> *Lower East Side –*

When a fire is set with kerosene, the whole street lights up orange. The building explodes. Its pieces come crashing down. Curled fingernails of paint, scraps of linoleum, they whirl, they drift down to earth, they lift suddenly into the air, they float away on the currents that fire creates. It's a fire-ballet. The roof groans open to the sky.

All night the firemen's water pours through the building, out its blackened entry, and down the stoop in a massive cascade. By morning it's frozen solid, a rippling, baroque river of ice like a tongue too big for its mouth.

The building resists, but is forced to give up its intentions, its art, the art of holding.

It held the kitchen table where the kid did homework.
It held the floor the mother stood on while she cooked.

They were the last tenants, the holdouts, before the thirteenth and final fire.

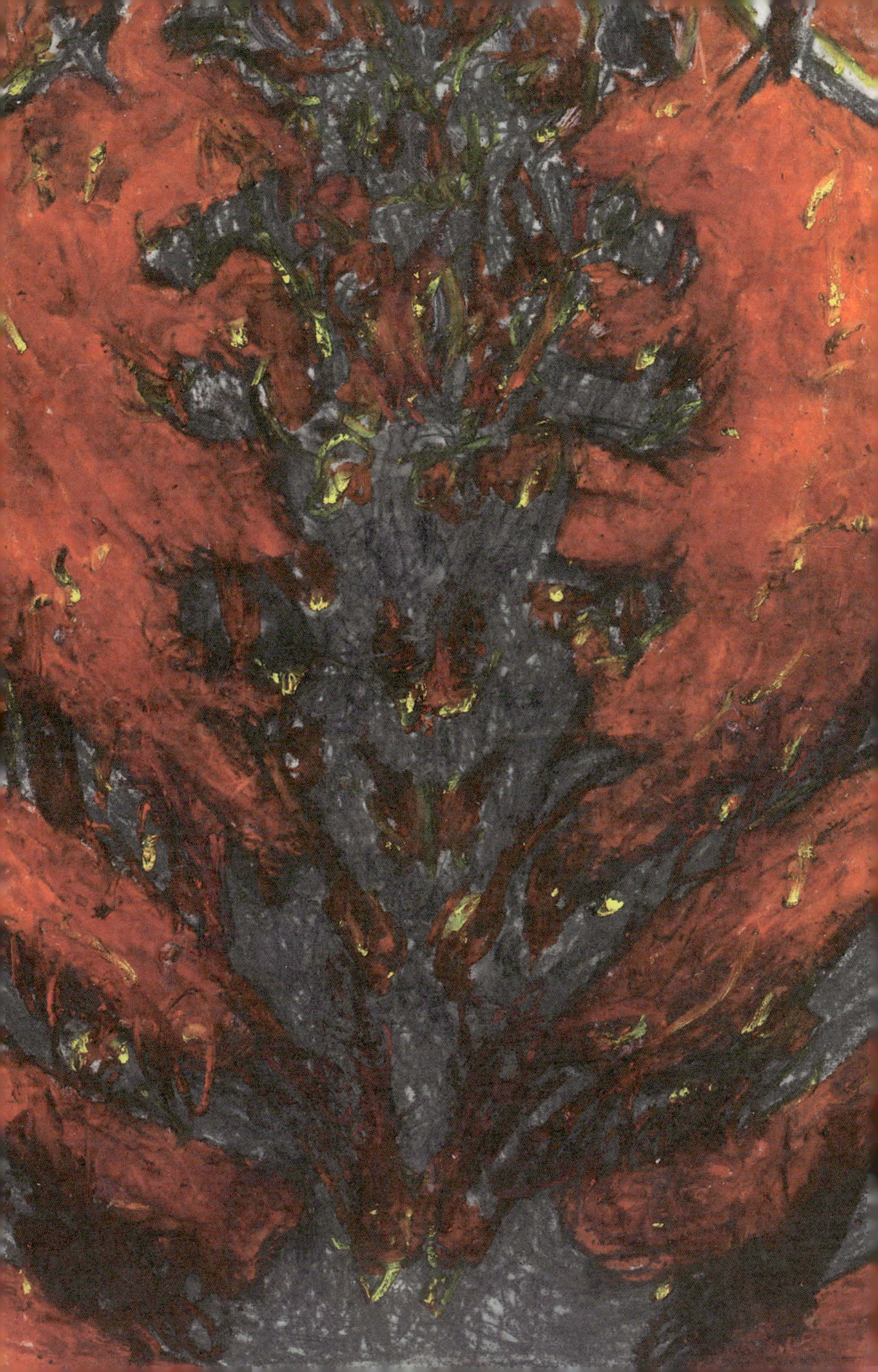

Fritz stopped by frequently to rant at me.

God in Heaven, what did I do in my life to deserve this –

Demolition is the twin of building. Half of making is unmaking. Demolition is the forensics of fire but also of the life before it.

Pulling up the linoleum we find the shopping lists and the newspapers from the fifties, then the twenties, then the first floorboards with pencil calculations scribbled on them. Under plaster and lath, in chalk, perfectly preserved till I touched it, one workman in 1889 showed another how to write "kosher."

Guys would find me kneeling over some fragment of book or shoe.

"What's with you and this junk?"
"I got a feeling for this junk."
It was my ritual and my religion.

In the apartments we find blackened pots on the stove, tables set, homework books open. They left that fast when the fire came.

The kid at the table, the mom at the stove.
She scooped that kid up while the beans were simmering, while long division was mid-number.
They ran out into the street in winter.

I committed myself to them,
that they should find safety,
That they should be held.

The Hemlock Society charter vacation

Fritz, the composer of epic notes, thundering Wagnerian letters, elegies, purple epistles. He kept stacks of yellow legal paper for this purpose on his desk.

One summer day when I was in my twenties my friend EA, a poet, an older woman Fritz had never met, but who had spoken to him on the phone the many times that he had called her house looking for me, asked,

> "How is your father?"

"He's OK."

> "You sure he's not sick?"

"No, why?"

> "You sure he's not having some kind of mental breakdown? I got an unusual letter from him."

I went to her house and read the letter.

Dear EA, I must first introduce myself,

as we have only met by telephone.

I am Fritz Bermann, Karen's father.

I would not write to you like this, purely out of the blue,

if it were not for urgent and extraordinary circumstances

with which you – and only you – can help me.

I have been diagnosed with a rare and fatal blood disease.

My doctors tell me there is no hope that I will be saved,

because the cure is very particular and really one-in-a-million.

They have searched the world over for a donation of blood,

a transfusion of a very rare and particular type of blood,

a transfusion of which would save me.

They have, as I say, searched the world over,

and have found that you, EA, are the only person on earth

with the right kind of blood.

Only an immediate transfusion of your blood, EA,

can save me from virtually certain death.

Please contact me immediately at this number

so that we may arrange to meet for a transfusion.

I repeat that my need is extremely urgent.

"WHAT?" I said.
She smiled.

> "Ah. I see. He's speaking metaphorically.
> 'Mark but this flea, and mark in this,
> How little that which thou deniest me is … '"

"WHAT?"

> "You don't know John Donne?
> Your father is clearly very well-versed in
> the tradition of erotic metaphysical poetry."

"He definitely is NOT," I said, picturing him in
his spotty undershirt.

My father had got it right, had sniffed out the lurid
quality that would appeal to her. The odds of them
being complementary lunatics? I was dizzy.

Dear EA,

It is three weeks and I have not received a response from you.

Every day as I confront the empty mailbox

my heart grows weaker, as if the poison in my blood

were growing stronger.

Surely you, a poet,

can understand my desperate need

<u>of a transfusion from you</u> – of your healthy living blood,

flowing like a merry river, sparkling with oxygen …

Fritz wrote an elegy to his dog when it died and
hung it prominently on the living room wall
along with a picture of the dog.

If there is a heaven for good dogs –

My mother, when she died, received the same treatment.

Your daughters watched over you
like two stars in the firmament –

He loved the word FIRMAMENT.
The dog, my mother, they whirled together in the firmament.
He also loved the word WHIRL, which I had clarified
for him many years earlier in the course of a conversation
about why he and my mother stayed together despite
their, and our, crushing misery.

"Dad, don't you ever say you stayed together for
the sake of the children. We think it would be better
if you got a divorce."

You know the story about how before God –
He-Who-Does-Not-Exist – said "Let there be light,"
and then organized things into their proper categories,
there was just chaos, original chaos?
Well, my marriage to your mother was whorling –
WHORLING – in that original chaos.

In response to this I had nothing.
I was nine years old.
I could only take a deep breath and say,

"You mean *whirling*, Dad."

Teddy, an old Viennese friend of my father's, died suddenly.
"I'm really sad," I cried, and I put my arm around Fritz's neck.
He didn't react – didn't even turn his head to look at me.
He looked ahead stoically or deafly.
We walked to the funeral parlor in the terrible heat.
He wore a light blue short-sleeved shirt over his undershirt.
"Dad, shouldn't you wear at least a jacket?
You look like a workman."

I AM a workman.

We got into the funeral parlor and stood around dumbly
while men in suits and women who had just come from the
hairdressers chatted. My father left my side and worked his
way through the crowd to Teddy's wife, Betty. She was surrounded
by people and was talking in her usual loud animated way,
though this day with a stricken face.

"Fritz!" she cried when she saw him.

He went up to her and put one paw on her back.
She leaned against him and put her arms around his neck
and her face against his shirt. He held her and stood
absolutely still while she cried on his shirt. He did not pat her,
or back off to look into her face, or say "I'm so sorry,"
or "You'll be OK," or "He was a great guy," or anything at all.
He just stood there in the noisy crowd, holding her with
the patience of an animal.

I say to Fritz, "Listen, it's important. We need to know. When you die, do you want to be buried or cremated?"

> *What are you bothering me? What's it to me?*
> *Put me in the landfill on Staten Island.*

Or

> *Kid, that will be your problem.*

Once he said,

> *I think I would like to be buried ...*
> *But wait a minute. There are no cemeteries near here.*
> *I'd have to go way out on Long Island, and how would you kids get there?*

"We'd drive, Dad."

> *You don't have cars.*

"But YOU have a car, Dad." (A long pause.)

"Dad, are you telling me you won't let us drive your car even after you're dead?"

No, no, of course you can drive my car after I'm dead. I just want to be sure you're going to be very, very careful with it.

"I have a feeling you don't want us driving it even after you're dead."

Well, there's not exactly going to be anything I can do about it. I won't be able to stop you, will I?

"No, but it'll bother you!"

I'm sure I won't be thinking about it. In fact, I'm sure I won't be thinking about anything.

"Dad, I have a feeling that when it comes to car maintenance, you're still going to be thinking about it when you're dead."

I write up a document: "I, Fritz Bermann, give my children permission to drive my car after I am dead into all eternity." I ask him to sign and date it. He does so, sighing.

French Uncle Jacques went senile and immediately forgot what little English he had reluctantly accrued over a fifty-year period in the US. He spoke only French and a bit of Spanish and Italian from wartime.

In the eighth-floor apartment in Queens he sat quietly next to the body of the French kit plane, watching the trucks passing by on the Throgs Neck Bridge.

When he lay dying in a Jewish nursing home in Flushing, I heard my father and my aunt conspiring on the telephone to keep their older brother Leo, the religious Jew, away.

My father said,

I told him Jacques was in no shape for visitors.
If you can be there all afternoon today,
I can be there all afternoon tomorrow.

"What's this about?" I asked him.

None of your business.

"What the hell?"

Well … I suppose you kids are old enough to know. Jacques isn't Jewish.

"WHAT?"

And therefore I don't want my brother there with him alone.

"WHAT?"

Because my brother has some suspicion, he's always thought something was fishy about Jacques as a Jew, even a French Jew. My brother is a snoopy bastard. I don't make it above him OR beyond him to sneak in there to lift up the blanket while Jacques is laying there unconscious, to look at his penis.

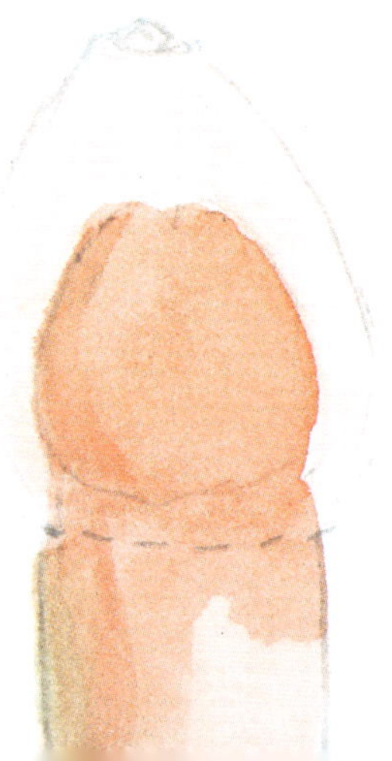

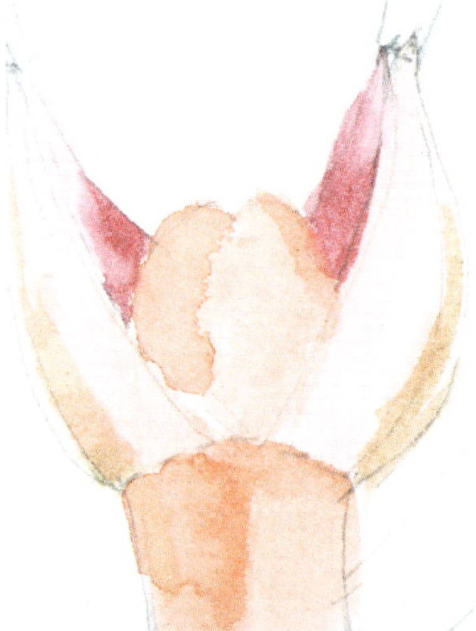

"WHAT?"

> *Of course Jacques isn't circumcised, what do you think?*

Then Jacques died, and they were even more anxious.

"But he's in the morgue now, Dad, in one of those cold lockers. Leo has no access to his body."

> *You don't know my brother. He has connections, rabbi connections, all over the city. I don't make it beyond him to get one of his rabbi cronies to slip into the morgue at Flushing General to lift the sheet and take a look.*

There was great haste, then, to get Jacques buried.
When it turned out to be much cheaper to have him cremated,
they were delighted, though this too would create
a problem in the family.

He called me that day with relief in his voice.

> *It's done. Finito.*

"The evidence has been destroyed?"

> *Ashes. For all eternity.*

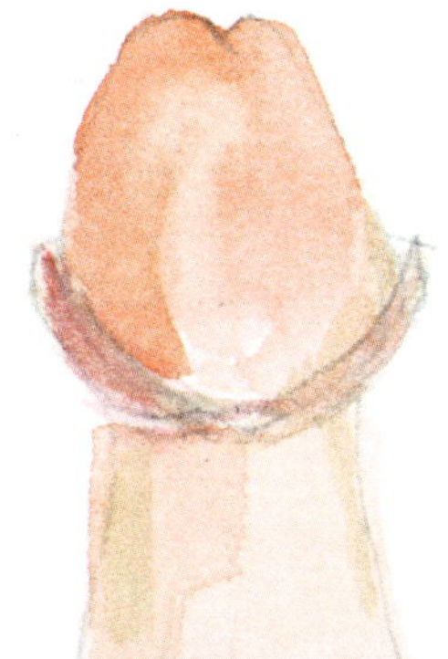

Fritz decided to cut off contact with his older brother, Leo.

"Dad, this is so sad … at this age, with so little time left,
after all you've been through, after all the losses, you
want to lose your brother too, you choose to lose
your brother too? You want to die at war
with your brother?
Don't you want to die at peace with him?
Don't you want to die at peace, period?"

I'm not at war! Do I look like I'm at war?
In this undershirt?
I just don't want to talk to my brother
ever again. I reject his religious bullshit
and his existence.
And I feel very peaceful about it.
This is how I am going to die at peace.

Later on, he had to do the same with his sister in South Africa, to break with her, because of a fight they had over saying goodbye at the airport.

"Dad. OK. I understand that not forgiving your brother had to do with moral principles plus other *mishegas*. But now you are having a serious fight with Elsa over what – saying goodbye at the airport?
And not forgiving her?
You might never see her again!"

Right! And that would be fine with me.

"Your sister was already disowned once
by your father and brother.
You didn't see her for thirty-five years!"

Of course I haven't forgotten the past.
Kid, we all had tough lives, she doesn't have
exclusive rights to a tough life.

"You sure about this?
You sure this is going to feel good?"

Yes. It's going to feel very good.

"How could you?"

How could I? Easy. She wanted to come back to the
car and say goodbye to Dora. I said, depends on
how crowded it is where I'm double-parked.
So she comes back, they start into a long goodbye,
and then I see – a cop! He's giving tickets
to the standing cars!

So I say, "Elsa! I gotta go!"
She says, "One more minute!"
I say, "No minutes! You want me to get a ticket?
No thank you!"
She and Dora are still carrying on
but I gotta pull away.
I'm sorry, but what does she know about the cost of
a traffic ticket at JFK? A fortune! I could fly
her to South Africa for the price of a ticket.

"She says you were brutal about it."

Brutal? I'll give you brutal. You want to know
what's brutal? Brutal is a ticket you get from
a cop at JFK.

A letter from his sister found after his death explained more:

Dear Fritz,
I should not have been surprised by your violent behavior
at the airport when I attempted to say goodbye to my sister,
who only God knows when I will see again.
You're the same person you were at eight years of age,
savage, tearing apart my dolls, smashing their heads.
And you won't listen to anybody.
It's in your own interest to let me give you advice about
how to improve your table manners.
But no, you push me aside roughly,
so you can go on eating with the food
half-in-half-out of your mouth,
shoveling it in with any implement available,
speaking and shouting while your lips
and chin are covered with food – in this too
you are still the chaotic boy you were in Vienna,
and nobody could teach you anything,
and you wonder and complain that
our father had to beat you?
It was the only language you understood.

To die at peace was to die at war.

The story of Grandma Melanie's broken-hearted bohemian painter-lover was one of the stories Fritz and his friends told like mantras as they sat at home in Rego Park or Flushing or in the Giant Pickle Diner, stories about people from the Other World, the world before the war, about thwarted destinies, eternal searches, miraculous recoveries, relationships lost and found, or found and lost, people who appeared in the hallways of old-age homes right here in Queens, or at the edge of the Grand Canyon, in a restaurant in Florence, or at an airport on the way home to Australia.

They told these stories during the *jause*, the Austrian afternoon gathering of infinite sweet-and-salty little plates, over coffee cake, pound cake, giant stale Danish, wet prunes and fruit compote, strange deviled eggs, mixtures called "salads" with mayonnaise and chopped pickles and minced cold cuts, sugar-free mocha cakes, coral-pink sauces and trembling gelatinous mysteries I refused to eat, and weak coffee from the Endless Coffee coffee pot, or from the big percolator, or *staub* (dust), which was my name for the off-brand instant coffee they pronounced acceptable, or tea from teabags of various provenances.

"What, did you carry this box of teabags with you when you crossed the Red Sea?"

That tea is perfectly good!

"Do you want real coffee or *staub?*"

As long as it's hot. And put some milk in it.

"Do you mean real milk or fake milk?"

As long as it's white.

While putting Swiss cheese on a bagel my father says,

> *So I assume the rest of you also got papers*
> *from the consulate in the last few weeks?*

Papers from the Austrian consulate and how to deal with them are regular topics of conversation and debate in this group.

Susanna says, "Yes, I already returned them."

My father turns to Liesl. *What about you?*

Liesl replies, "Yes, I received them, but you know how I feel about that."

> *I know how you feel, and I think you're making*
> *a big mistake.*

"How do you feel?" I ask her.

Liesl replies, "I have never accepted reparations."

"Why not?"

> "Because in order to receive reparations I have to fill out the forms. I have to look at those pieces of paper written in German in that terrible German typeface. I have to register with the authorities. I have done all that enough in my lifetime. I don't want to be inside any of their systems again. I don't want them to know my name, my age, where I live; I don't want them giving me any more numbers."

"I can understand that," I say.

Marta, adjusting her ancient cleavage, says:

"I can't. I think you're totally crazy.
In fact, I have already given Henry instructions
that I should be kept alive as long as possible,
I don't care what the circumstances are. For instance,
if I am lying in a hospital brain-dead, he is never
to pull the plug. I want to be kept on life support
as long as possible. Give me everything they got,
all the tubes and machines. I don't care how dead I am,
just keep my heart beating so that the bastards
have to keep on paying."

Fritz says:

I don't feel that way,
I'm preparing for the Hemlock Society charter vacation.

Then all of a sudden it began

Before my father flies, he calls me:

> *Remember I bought my tickets with American Express.*
> *That means two million in insurance if I go down.*

"Are you going on your Hemlock Society charter vacation?"

> *Sorry, honey, not yet.*

Our best death plan so far is this:
A chartered plane, a remote unpopulated location,
pilot, crew, and passengers all ancient and all
members of the Hemlock Society.
All on board, so to speak.
Everyone will be happy.

But seriously:
"Weren't you going to Hemlock Society meetings, Dad?
Don't they prepare you with good ways?"

> *I tried those Hemlock people, but I didn't like them.*
> *They're obsessed with death.*

"That's the point, Dad."

> *Yes, but in such a boring way! How much can you*
> *talk about plastic bags? They lack humor. If I have to*
> *drive the Major Deegan to get there, I expect it to be*
> *more interesting.*

He was not too worried about how it would go.

Don't worry, honey, if I get sick enough,
I'll take control, I'll just kill myself.

"How will you kill yourself?"

I'll jump out the window.

"Dad, no! You have to have a better plan than that!"

It's not so easy!
Too bad you made me get rid of that
little gun of mine!

"A gun is also not a good plan, Dad."

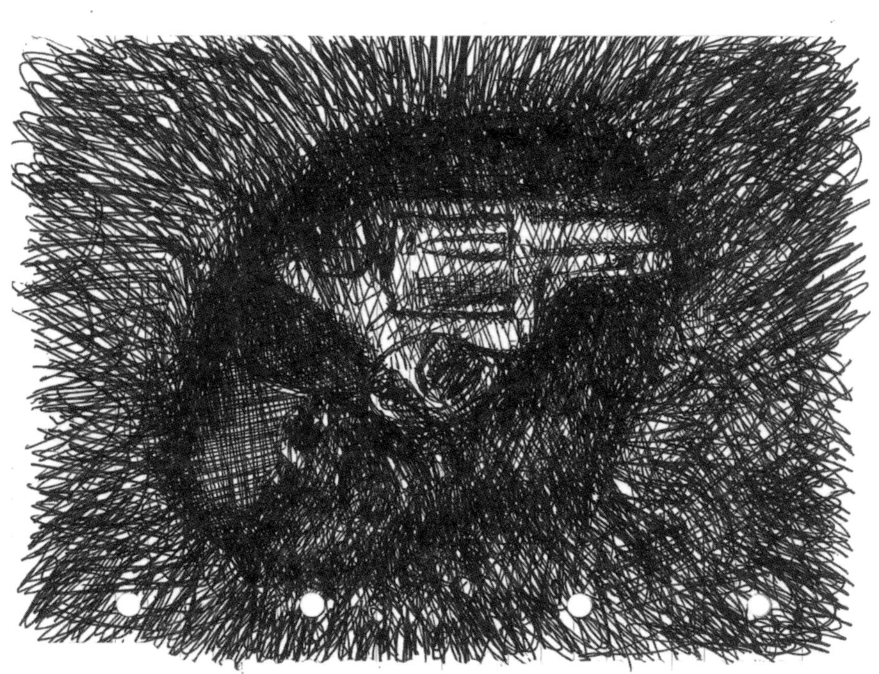

We joked about death like that until the last minute.
We were sure it would all work out somehow.
That he, that we, would not be rendered
helpless and suffering.
Well, almost the last minute.

For a long time he had no aches and pains.

> *How is it that my friends got so old?*
> *I myself feel like a young man. No more than forty.*
> *And when I was forty, I felt immortal.*

He was so alive, he was pink, sometimes red.
He was "bursting." He was "bursting with life."
He wore shirtsleeves in winter. Life was shooting
through his pores, very hot.
He climbed eleven floors carrying the baby in a stroller
when the elevators were broken, no problem.
He climbed the rocks of the Palisades singing Beethoven
at high volume.

The bombing, the flattening, the killing them all
one to a hundred, yes, we were used to that.
Bursting.

But suicide? Never.
Death itself was unthinkable because
he felt that his existence was fundamental
to the existence of the entire universe.
It was his job to know it and to narrate it.
His voice, and Beethoven, at high volume.

Then all of a sudden it began.

I have been where you have not been

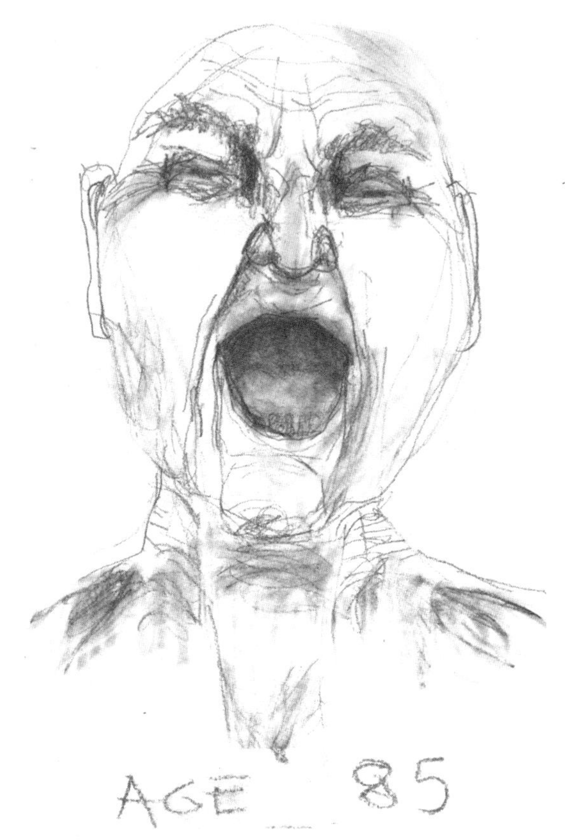

My phone buzzed.

Get here immediately. There's an emergency.

"What kind of emergency?"

It's a very urgent emergency.

"I mean, what is the emergency?"

Get here now!

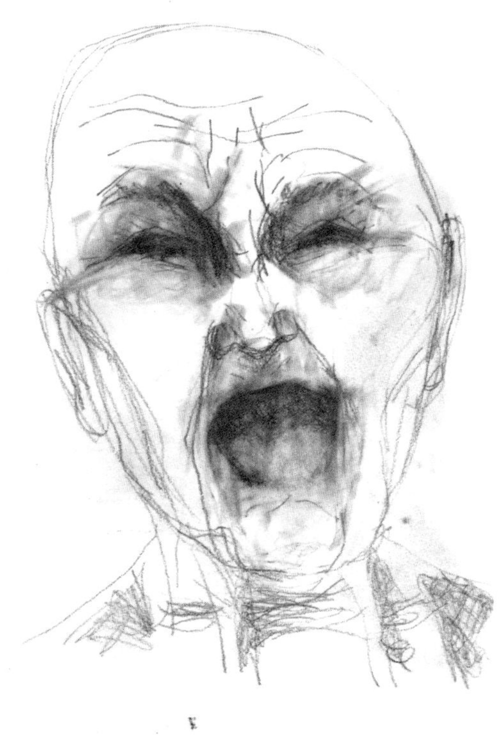

AGE 90

“What’s the emergency?”

The emergency is I am old!

“That’s not an emergency, Dad.”

It is!

He was right, of course.

"What are you going to do today, Dad?"

I think I'm going to jump out the window.

"Don't do that, Dad, you'll traumatize Juan."
(The doorman, whom we loved.)

What do I care about Juan?

"Well, then, you'll traumatize me."

You're already plenty traumatized, a little more
won't matter.

"Yes it will."

You'll get over it. When are you coming home?
If you're not here within two hours,
I'm going to kill myself.

"Dad, I'm already on the E train."

Good. And I hope I'm dead when you get here.

"Wait! I'm bringing brownies."

Are they any good?
Don't bring me the dry, boring kind.

"You know I wouldn't."

We'll see. If I get up the courage, I'll kill myself.
If I don't, I'll eat brownies with you.
And they better be good.

He fell and was taken to the hospital.

You have abandoned me in this terrible place.
Ich bin in der HÖLLE –

"You're speaking German, Dad – "

I am?
I'm in HELL.
I'm in HELL and it's your fault.
If you don't come to New York in the next hour,
I'm going to kill myself.

"How are you planning to kill yourself in a hospital?"

Don't worry about it. That's my business.

Rehüber, Rehober …

"Rehab?"

Oh yes, that's the word. Rehab.
There is no rehab going on in this place.
It's a camp. And I don't mean a summer camp.
You don't know half about this place.
It's a criminal place.
I'd kill them one to a hundred. And you can say
that I'm insane. Fine. I don't blame you
for not understanding.
But I have been where you have not been.

Ihr werdet mich nicht im Gefängnis einsperren!
Ich schwöre daß ich eine Bombe baue, und diesen
Ort ins Jenseits befördere!
I'm going to build a bomb and blow up this
entire godforsaken building and everyone in it!

The director called me to her office.

"Mrs. Bermann – "
(What was I, his mother?
In the principal's office in Vienna, 1931?)
"How long has he been like this?"

I could not answer.

"I'm sorry, but we can't keep him here.
We can't have yelling about bombing and killing.
This is a care facility."

French Uncle Jacques had a companion in the Resistance who
couldn’t crack the vial of cyanide and so committed suicide
when he was trapped on the top floor of a building
by throwing himself into the stairwell.

We heard about a woman who escaped by floating across the ocean holding onto a basketball. Another who hid inside a cow.

Can these stories be true?

I have listened for so long that to me
everything is believable.
Since things happened that I could not have imagined,
anything I imagine can happen.
I look into flower vases and drinking straws to see
if anyone is hiding inside.

The possible and the actual,
one sits inside the other,
like an organ inside the body.

Since things happened that I could not
have imagined any thing I can imagine can
happen. I look inside flower vases and
drinking straws to see if anyone is hiding inside.

He left no note.

I was glad that, finally, he had spoken till
he was finished.

I didn't want a note.
I didn't want another fucking word.

The last time I saw him he turned away
when it was time to say goodbye.

The drop

The drop was forty-five feet max.

Forty-one seven.
A maintenance man is never without a tape measure.

He'd have taken the flashlight out of his deep pants pocket

a maintenance man is never without a flashlight

for a better view of the ground below.

If You think I'm going to ask for Your help at this point
You've got another thing coming

Shaking his fist at the sky.

He'd dragged pieces of furniture over to the railing
so he could clamber up to a satisfactory height
from which he could launch, not just flop.
Maybe he was afraid that if he just flopped
he'd get hung up in the railing somehow,
and he wanted to clear it properly.

Maybe he thought it was undignified to flop.
Or maybe, and these all run together, really, he wanted,
he needed a certain heroic violence, a certain rageful
Greek tragedy violence, that suicide by falling carries
anyway but suicide by falling that begins with thrust,
upward and outward, which first expresses a defiant
belief in flight, a defiant belief in going out by going
up, an extra grim kick to the act, a tiny extra Fuck You,
though there was no one there to see it except for
God-who-does-not-exist and whom he hated violently.
– As if he were shot from a rocket, or a bomb, with
a propulsive and explosive force, a capacity to create
damage so much greater than a fall.
Anything can fall. A leaf can fall.
With the launch he could say *Yes*, or in his case
more likely *No, no more of this shit*, pounding his fist
on the table. The launch was the pounding fist.

After all the violence of his life I wanted him to fade out
in a garden, maybe under a tree.
That, I thought, would be a nice scene that could be
described at a memorial.
"And at the end he became so peaceful, etcetera ..."
"... kvelling in the love of his children, the beautiful
garden, the seven-layer cake, the therapy dogs, the
tight uniforms of the nurses, etcetera ..."

There was an unopened box of chocolate chip cookies
on the kitchen counter.
Unopened? Are you kidding?
Since when could he resist?

I want to say,
Dad, get the fuck down from there.
Go into the kitchen, make yourself a cup of *staub*,
sit down and open the goddamn box of cookies.
That's the dad we wanted.
But that's not the dad we got.
We got the flying and falling dad, the one who went.
With grim resolve, or with tears, but he went.

Couldn't you have become a sweet old man
sitting in a garden, maybe under a tree?
Couldn't you have given us the *nachas* of caring for you
in your oldness?
Wasn't the *nachas* of our existence,
our accomplishments, our love,
wasn't that enough for you?

But of course it wasn't,
you fucking break-the-backbone-of-your-resistance dad –

"Did he ever talk about killing himself?"

Yes, he did, all the time.

"And what, you didn't think he was serious?"

How we got through

AS IF is how we got through, us kids.

As if, contrary to everything we'd been taught,
every day were not an emergency
As if when we left the house we would
almost certainly return
As if the footsteps on the stairs
were just neighbors
As if the neighbors could be trusted
As if we had choices
As if we could afford to have hopes
As if our hopes might not be thwarted
As if we had futures, lives ahead of us.

Going to the supermarket
As if it were not the last day on earth
Is how we got through.

You who have emerged from the flood—

Really, how could it have been any other way.
Now I see that it was written from the beginning.

"At least he's at peace now," others said.

To which I could only say,
"Are you fucking kidding?"

First of all, he's not anything now.
But if he is anything now,
He is raging still.

You who have emerged from the flood—

What a magnificent panorama 2

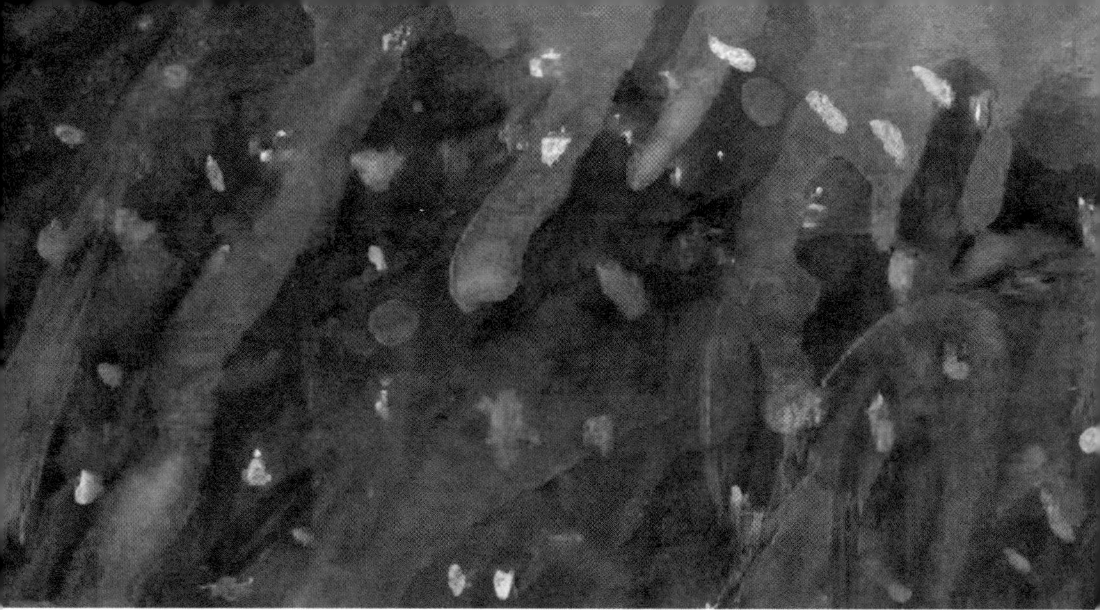

In the morning I say to him, "I think I'll go see
the new Holocaust Museum downtown."
I am surprised when he says, *I'll go with you.*

"You will? Why? You don't like museums."

This one is different. It's a beautiful museum.

I am so pleased that he wants to come out of the house that I decide not to ask questions. We head downtown on the subway and arrive at Battery Park around noon.

1. On the first floor, he walks ahead of me quickly, not looking around, and waits at the end, by the stairway to the second floor. After fifteen minutes he comes back.
At the rate you're going, we'll be here all day.
Ten minutes later he comes back again.
You know, rush hour starts soon.

2. On the second floor is a history of antisemitism and the Holocaust. He waves his hand dismissively.
This we know about. Germans.
He goes to the stairway.

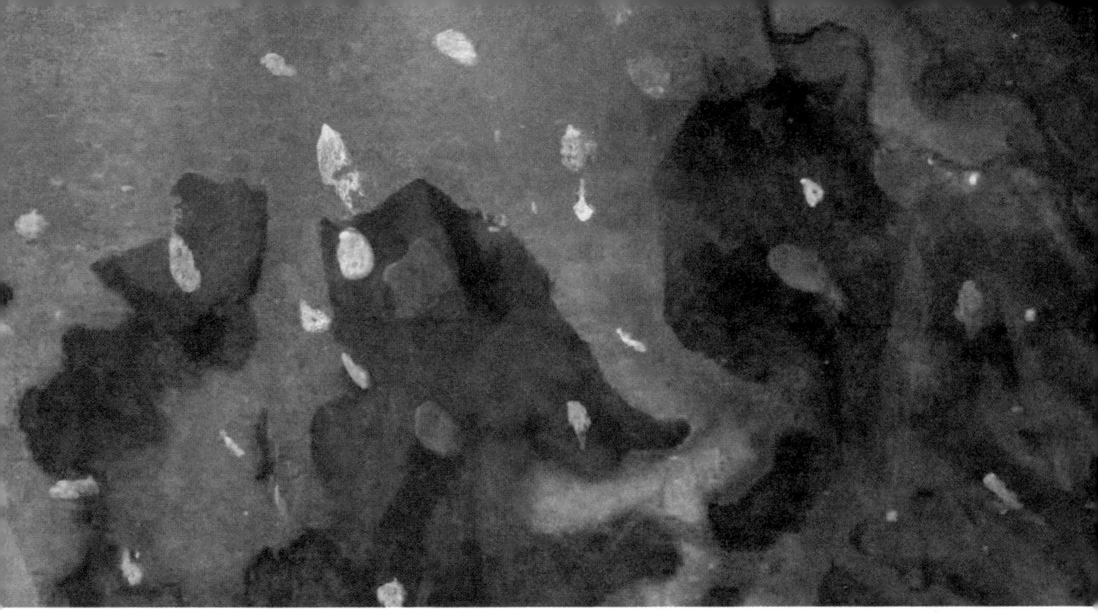

3. On the third floor he enjoys an excellent cookie and cup of coffee and explains the view to me.

> *You can see all of New York Harbor from this spot.*
> *There is the Statue of Liberty. Next to it is Ellis Island …*

These things are in plain sight, so I am about to say
"I know, I see them," but instead I say,
"Wow! What a magnificent panorama!"

4. We go outside and sit in the sun on the giant rocks
that make up the memorial garden.
He blinks upward. He says,

> *What a gorgeous sky!*

and

> *It's incredible that we can sit here in this*
> *splendid place for free!*

and

> *You look very nice today! You are wearing a*
> *very nice skirt!*

and

> *There are moments in which you feel you have already*
> *ascended to paradise.*

The cookies

Oh, these are terrible cookies.
You can tell even before you open this lousy package.
He would have been very disappointed in these cookies.
But I'm sure there's nothing else chocolatey in the house.
So – in a time of need, and this is definitely such a time –

I guess I could eat one.